First published in 2006 by New Holland Publishers (UK) Ltd
London • Cape Town • Sydney • Auckland
Garfield House, 86–88 Edgware Road, London W2 2EA, United Kingdom
www.newhollandpublishers.com
80 McKenzie Street, Cape Town 8001, South Africa
14 Aquatic Drive, Frenchs Forest, NSW 2086, Australia
218 Lake Road, Northcote, Auckland

ISBN 1 84537 104 6
10 9 8 7 6 5 4 3 2 1

Editorial Direction: Rosemary Wilkinson Senior Editor: Clare Hubbard Production: Hazel Kirkman
Designed and created for New Holland by AG&G Books Copyright © 2004 "Specialist" AG&G Books
Design: Glyn Bridgewater Illustrations: Dawn Brend, Gill Bridgewater, Coral Mula and Ann Winterbotham
Editor: Alison Copland Photographs: see page 80
Reproduction by Pica Digital Pte Ltd, Singapore
Printed and bound in Malaysia by Times Offset (M) Sdn. Bhd.

The information in this book is true and complete to the best of our knowledge. All recommendations
are made without guarantee on the part of the authors and the publishers. The authors and publishers
disclaim any liability for damages or injury resulting from the use of this information.

WATER GARDEN
Specialist

**The essential guide to designing,
building, planting, improving and
maintaining water gardens**

A. & G. Bridgewater

NEW HOLLAND

Contents

Author's foreword **2**

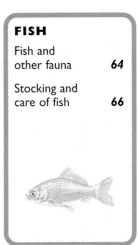

Author's foreword

Water is our most prized and precious possession. Not only is it essential to life itself, but it also has mysterious qualities that we find spiritually uplifting. At the very heart of our being, there is a need to see and feel water. Every year, hundreds of thousands of people travel vast distances just to experience what we consider to be special stretches of water. We are variously enthralled, silenced, inspired and sparked into creativity by ancient springs, holy wells, tumbling rivers, crashing waterfalls, eerie lakes and vast oceans.

Traditionally, humans had no choice other than to build their homes as near as possible to a reliable water source. Only the very wealthy were able to move bodies of water. A wealthy man did not have to bow to nature and live in a damp river valley – he could build his house on top of a hill, and then set about moving water to suit his needs. Water gardens, complete with artificial lakes, diverted rivers and pumping stations, became status symbols. Today, new technology, such as flexible liners, PVC piping and electric pumps, make everything possible.

If you have dreams about building your own water garden, on whatever scale, this book will gently guide you through all the finger-tingling stages, from choosing a project, selecting tools and making drawings through to digging holes, building walls, planting, stocking with fish and much more. No more fantasizing about water gardens: now is the time to create one of your own.

Plant names

For the sake of universal clarity and comprehension, current recommended botanical names for plants are given throughout this book; when more familiar botanical names, or even more friendly traditional common names, are still used, these are also included.

Safety

Many of the projects and procedures are potentially dangerous. Digging holes and working with electricity and tools are both, to some extent, dangerous. Because babies and toddlers are fascinated by water, if you have small children, or children visit you, you must NEVER leave them unaccompanied.

MEASUREMENTS

In this book, both metric and imperial measurements are given – for example, 1.8 m (6 ft) – but very few of the measurements are critical.

Water-garden style

There are many styles of water garden: classical, Italian, Islamic, modern, naturalistic and so on. Though you may have preconceived notions – the garden has to be formal, or there should be lots of plants and fish – you must take into account the location, size and character of your home and garden. The finished water garden will of necessity be a coming-together of your imaginings and what you actually have on the ground.

How can I pick a style?

FORMAL AND INFORMAL

A formal water garden is defined by the way its highly visible geometrical shape relates to the size, shape and character of the house. By contrast, a natural water garden is built so that it is indistinguishable from the real thing.

A formal water garden complete with symmetrically placed items such as steps, lawns, planters and walls. All the details are strictly straight-edged and geometrical; even the waterlilies are in rows.

Although this fairly new water garden is still somewhat rigid in form, it has been designed so that, when the plants grow and intermingle, it will have a natural, informal appearance.

THEMES

While there are only two basic styles of water garden – natural and architectural, or informal and formal – within these two groupings there are many options. For example, if you want a natural garden, you could have a garden based on a meadow stream, or a bend in a river, or a beach, or an exotic island … there are many options within the chosen style.

Inspired by great paintings

If you love paintings by artists like Claude Monet or Paul Gauguin, who featured water gardens in their work, you could simply use one of your favourite paintings as a master plan. What could be better than a garden based on one of Monet's lily-pond paintings, or a beach garden based on a painting by Gauguin?

Inspired by plants

A good idea, if plants inspire you, is to list your favourites and then work towards building a water garden that encompasses all their needs. For example, if you are fond of irises, rushes and grasses, a slow meandering stream with large areas of bog on the side would be a good choice. Be mindful, when actually planting in the water, that you must, for good water quality, achieve a balance between the amounts of oxygen and algae.

Assessing the impact

You must consider carefully how the project will affect your friends and family. Will your children or grandchildren be at risk? Will the sound of running water upset your neighbours? Will you have the time and energy to keep the garden in good order?

Fish

If you want to have fish, the size and character of the body of water is all-important. Although it is relatively easy to introduce native fish to a natural pond, and then simply let native frogs and newts join in the fun, it is not so easy to keep fish in a formal, plant-free pond.

Assessing your garden

Will my plot be big enough?

Although in many ways a minute yard in a city is more of a challenge than a large country plot, the truth is that, no matter the size of your garden, there will be a design to suit. The best way forward is to spend time in your garden and in various inspirational gardens – planning, dreaming and weighing up the possibilities – and then aim for a design that is a balanced, logical and harmonious blend of what you have and what you desire.

There are options for every type of garden. Left: a high-quality water feature for a Japanese garden. Centre: a cascade pool for a small town garden. Right: a natural pond for a large country garden.

THINKING ABOUT YOUR SPACE

Walk around your garden at various times throughout the day and week – mornings, lunchtime, when there is a sunset, on weekdays and weekends, and in various weather conditions – and consider carefully the space and location, and how the type, time and character of the day affects actual space and perceived space. For example, a small garden in the city might well feel more spacious in the evenings and weekends when the hustle and bustle has ceased. In the country, the traffic flow at peak times might mean that you only want to use that part of the garden that is furthest away from the road. You may have room for a large natural water garden, but a small, high-walled courtyard with a carefully chosen water feature might be a better option.

Ask yourself some questions. Do you want to turn the whole space into a water garden with the walls, planting and trees being integrated and inter-related? Or do you want a single, small area set aside, in much the same way as you might have a room in your home set aside for a single activity? Will the sound of moving water be a problem when you are lying in bed, or do you enjoy that sound?

Consider also how the space will be used by friends and family – your partner, the neighbours, relations, children, the dog, and all the rest. Will a large pond be a problem if you have children? Do you have a large dog that is going to jump in the pond, get in a mess and pad mud throughout the house? Look at existing trees. Are falling leaves or shade going to be a problem? Spend time in the garden, quietly standing or perhaps sitting in your favourite corner. Look around, at the road, the boundary walls and fences, at your neighbours' windows, at overhead cables, at the various paths that cross the garden, and so on. Try to take everything into account.

Perhaps a small self-contained feature is all you need.

A simple water feature – perhaps no more than a good-sized pond with a bridge over it – can completely transform a boring garden.

Opportunities

One person's difficulties are another person's opportunities. The trick here is to look at your site – the slope of the ground, the aspect and the soil conditions – and then as far as possible work with what you have. For example, do not necessarily think of rocky ground as being a problem, but rather think of the stone waste as being useful.

• If your site is sloping, you could have a fast-running stream, or perhaps a series of stepped ponds and terraces with interlinked waterfalls.

• If your site is as flat as a pancake, you could have a large, calm pond.

• If the soil is damp, you could have lots of areas of bog garden.

• If you have interesting walls between gardens – such as brick, stone or flint – you could use them as a backdrop for such things as formal ponds and wall masks.

• If you have left-over materials, rubble, stone or concrete, you could use these as backfill for raised ponds and structures.

• If you finish up with a large pile of earth, you could model and reshape the contours of your garden.

Problems

Building water gardens can be fraught with problems, some of them big but most of them small. The best idea is to approach them head on, and either to work round them and modify your designs accordingly or to figure how you can remove or solve the problem.

• If your site is extremely sloping, for example too much of a slope to walk up, you may have to think in terms of cutting a terrace or even creating a series of waterfalls.

• If you are blessed with a large area of concrete, such as the base of an old shed, you could use it as a foundation for a raised formal pond or perhaps a linked patio.

• If you have a very young family, meaning babies and toddlers, and you are worried about their safety, you could either hold back until they are older, or you could build the water garden and make sure that you train the children in all aspects of water safety.

• If you have a garden surrounded by large, mature trees, you could create a bog garden, perhaps with small water features rather than ponds.

• If the ground is almost completely rocky, you may have to think in terms of raised, formal ponds.

Water-garden guidelines

Water movement Water movement can only be achieved by the use of a pump. The best method is to place the pump in a sump or reservoir, and to pump the water up to a higher level so that it can flow back down towards the sump. You will need a source of electricity.

Sump

Size and shape Although the size and shape of your site will decide the size and shape of your pond, the choice of liner is also a primary factor. While preformed liners may look to be the easiest option, they are small, rather predictable in shape and difficult to install. Flexible liners, on the other hand, can be as big as your budget, allowing you to build a water garden of any shape and size.

Rocky stream

Plants Plants require sunlight and varying depths of water. Locate and design the pond so that there is plenty of sunlight and so that it steps down from side to centre.

Planting shelf in a pond

Fish Very roughly, the fish-to-pond ratio is 2.5 cm (1 in) of fish length to every hand-sized area of water surface. The best way to stock a pond is to start with the plants, leave it for a year, and then gradually follow on with the fish.

Goldfish

Maintenance The secret of having and keeping a successful water garden is not to wait until the fish start dying and the various channels and pumps start to clog up, but rather to have a regular maintenance programme. You will probably get muddy and wet from time to time, but that is all part of the fun.

Removing algae

TIPS FOR NEW GARDENERS

Making a start If you are a nervous beginner, start by drawing out designs for the whole garden, and then divide the work up into manageable chunks or phases. So you might build the main pond one year, put in a secondary pond the next year, and so on.

Pond size When it comes to designing a water garden, the cardinal rule is always go for the biggest possible pond or pool. A large, wide, shallow body of water is generally healthier, safer, easier to stock and maintain, and certainly more aesthetically pleasing, than a small, deep pool.

Have a clear vision Building and maintaining a water garden is undoubtedly a big commitment, not so much in money as in time and effort. For this reason, if you are at all undecided as to design and type, then you need to spend additional time simply viewing more gardens. Above all, you need to be enthusiastic and firm in your resolve.

Inspiration, passion and design

How do I proceed?

Successful water gardens are made up, in equal parts, of inspiration, passion and design. Most people begin by drawing inspiration from an experience – perhaps a wonderful garden that you visited, or a holiday when you sat by a lake, pool or well. Your passion is sparked into action, and you search out more gardens and start to visualize how yours might be. Finally, once you have carefully considered all the options and implications, you can start designing.

INSPIRATION AND PASSION

It is vital that, once you have been initially inspired, you go on to become passionate. Of course, inspiration and passion are not enough to hold the project together; you must harness these two feelings or emotions by channelling them into good, solid, well thought-out designs.

CHECKING OUT YOUR IDEAS

Once you are all fired up, then comes the perhaps more difficult task of checking out your ideas to make sure that they can realistically be brought to fruition. You might want a large pond, a formal pond, bog gardens and so on, but ask yourself the appropriate questions: is your site big enough, is the location right for what you have in mind, and can you afford it? You must start doing sums and then perhaps modify your ideas.

WHY DESIGN?

Good, solid design must follow on from inspiration and passion. You cannot just wander out into the garden in a dream state and start digging a hole – you must have an overall master design that guides your actions. Don't stick rigidly to one idea come what may, but be flexible. Don't be afraid to modify your ideas to suit changing needs. You might want a large, natural, meadow pond, but if your site is rocky and overhung with trees it might be a better idea to have a Japanese garden or a wild forest-glade garden. Try to incorporate everything in your design – your ideas, your bank balance and what you have on the ground.

There is something truly inspirational about a lily pond running riot – as the painter Claude Monet demonstrated.

If you like order and control, then perhaps a series of raised ponds is a good option, with flat water and restrained planting.

Guidelines for good design

Unlike a straightforward garden where you can chop and change everything as the mood takes you – the size of the lawn, the shape of the flower borders – a water garden with its fixed water features is less easy to change. The success of a water garden hinges on a whole mix of elements coming together.

Scale and shape The area of water needs to be as big as possible, but not so big that it feels uncomfortably large on the site or is dangerously close to the footings of the house. Regarding the choice between natural and geometrical shapes, a natural pond generally looks good just about anywhere but a formal, geometrical shape tends to look best when it is set in close proximity to the house.

Harmony and contrast While it is easy enough to create a natural-looking pond, one that very soon looks to be indistinguishable from the real thing, it is much more difficult to create a formal pond that looks and feels comfortable in any other position than close to the house. When a formal, geometrical pond is set close to the house, it must be considered from all aspects, and carefully aligned so that it is parallel to the house and related structures.

Continuing a theme Once you have opted for a theme, such as seaside, lakeside or Moorish, it is important that you follow through with appropriate planting and features.

Materials and techniques Although it is important that you use materials that are fitting and right for their purpose – local brick and stone – if you do decide to bring in boulders, marble or the like, then you must appreciate that there will of necessity be contrasts. You must also make sure that you are technically able to achieve your ends.

WATER-GARDEN OPTIONS AND STYLES

Formal garden pond

↘ Formal ponds can be created from either flexible or preformed liners used in conjunction with brick, wood, concrete and stone. While preformed shapes can technically be raised or set in the ground, they generally look their best when they are raised. Combinations of preformed shapes can be used to create more complex designs.

Natural garden pond

↗ Natural ponds are best created using flexible liners in conjunction with a totally concealed edging of block or brick and concrete.

Formal water garden

← Formal water gardens are characterized by geometrical shapes, crisp edges, vertical sides, tightly controlled planting and by being carefully aligned to the house and related paths, patios and terraces.

Natural stream garden

← A natural water garden including a stream needs to be built so that all the structures are hidden from view.

Japanese water garden

↗ Japanese water gardens are uniquely interesting and exciting options in that they are formal interpretations of nature. While the pond, stone edging, planting and raked gravel all look to nature for their inspiration, they are used in a formal, stylized way.

Water gardens for plants and fish

If your primary concerns are not so much with the shape and style of the water garden, nor with thoughts of informal versus formal, but are more to do with how much you are looking forward to having lots of plants and fish, then, almost by default, the best option is to have a natural water garden. You will need a large, wide pond with as much water surface as possible, and with the sides of the pond running down in a series of shallow steps and shelves – meaning from the sides through to the centre.

Plants and fish need plenty of sunlight. You can have areas of lightly dappled shade, but for the most part the pond must be in a sunny position. To a great extent, trees and ponds are a bad mix. Rotting leaves can be toxic, large trees cut out the sun, and the roots from trees can pierce the pond lining. While you can happily have well-trimmed, low-growing trees like willows at the side of the pond, it is definitely a bad idea to have the pond overhung with mature trees.

Planning and construction

Do I really need a master plan?

If you want the project to run smoothly, you must sort out everything – from who does what and when through to the order of work and what happens if it rains on the day when you are expecting delivery of concrete. If you plan everything out to the last detail, with drawings, lists and schedules, then not only will you get the job done with the minimum of sweat and stress, but along the way you will also probably have a lot of fun and enjoyment.

DECIDING WHAT TO KEEP

When you are planning a new water garden, do not be in a hurry to remove existing trees or large structures; it may be possible (or essential) to incorporate them into your design. If you do have to dig holes, cut down trees or remove structures, then do your utmost to reuse these materials.

MEASURING YOUR GARDEN

Start by drawing a rough plan (overhead view) of your existing garden. Measure the overall length of the boundaries, critical angles, the position of the house, the gate, other structures, trees and plants you want to keep, the position of the sun at various times throughout the day, and anything else that you think might affect the design. Record these items and measurements on your rough plan.

ADDITIONAL FEATURES REQUIRING PLANNING

Sometimes primary structures like bridges and decks are so complex in themselves that they need to have individual plans in their own right. For example, with a deck you must not only make drawings showing it in plan view, but you must also show all the critical details such as the leg-fixings in cross-section.

USEFUL CROSS-SECTIONS

Cross-section drawings show a 'sliced-through' view of a structure and can help you work out how a design should be built.

DRAWING A PLAN TO SCALE

After noting measurements on a rough plan (see right) redraw the plan accurately (to scale) on a sheet of graph paper. If the paper is divided into 1 cm (½ in) squares, you could use a scale of 1:50, where 1 cm (½ in) on the paper represents 50 cm (25 in) in the garden (divide all your measurements by 50). This is your basic plan which should not be drawn on again. Sketch out your ideas for the new

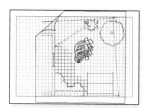

garden on photocopies of the basic plan. Once you have finalized the design, draw up a master plan by tracing over the top of the basic plan (tape the sheets of paper to a window so you can see through them and trace over lines). Use felt-tip pens or watercolours to colour in the plan and help you visualize planting schemes. If this sounds like too much hard work, try using a computer software design package.

PLANNING THE STRUCTURES

Decide where the primary structures need to go – the ponds, watercourses and sumps – and follow on with the secondary structures – the paths, steps, gates, power cable and pipes. Make sure along the way that you take everything into account. For example, if you have narrow paths and bridges, you must make sure that you can get the lawnmower and a wheelbarrow to all parts of the garden.

PLANTS AND FISH

If you particularly like bog plants or a special type of fish, make sure at the planning and construction stage that everything you have in mind to build is working towards that end. If the fish like calm but muddy waters and the plants need water-sodden, boggy ground, you have to ensure that your design is suitable.

WATER AND POWER SUPPLIES

Most ponds can be topped up using a hosepipe, but for a large pond you may want to install underground pipes and an automatic top-up system (see page 13). You will need professional help to install an electricity supply for running the pump and lights; alternatively, you could use low-voltage or solar power.

Planning checklist

- Have you finalized your design, including construction details?
- Have you made sure that your designs are not breaking any laws?
- Are your structures clear of underground pipes and cables?
- Do you need help from friends, relatives or professionals?
- Have you compared quotes for materials and services?
- Have you got the right tools?
- Have you set out the order of work?
- Have you found a way to protect fragile areas of the garden from repetitive over-walking?

POND LINING

Whatever your choice of pond lining (butyl or preformed), the secret of success is to make sure that the edges are completely concealed. The edges of preformed ponds are best covered with brick or pavers, while the edges of a flexible liner can be completely hidden underground. See how the various projects use different techniques to support and hide the edges.

A method of concealing butyl liner that gives the illusion of a natural pond.

FOUNDATIONS

Foundations and footings are the underground pads of concrete or compacted rubble that support the weight of paving, walls or other structures. The bigger the structure, the thicker and wider the foundations need to be.

WALLS

Formal ponds and other water features often need walls to retain water (these walls are made waterproof using a liner or tanking paint). Concrete blocks can be used where they will be hidden from view or rendered (coated with mortar) and bricks or stones are often chosen for their decorative effect. Mortar (see below) is used to join blocks, bricks or stones together.

STEPS

Steps need to be worked out on paper as a cross-section view. In a short flight of steps the depth ('going') and the height ('rise') of each step should be equal. The rise of a step must be no greater than 23 cm (9 in). To calculate the number of steps and the rise, divide the total height of the flight by 23 cm (9 in) and round upwards. Include foundations and start building from the bottom step.

MATERIALS

Materials can be obtained from dedicated bulk suppliers, DIY stores, builder's merchants and reclamation yards. A selection of the most useful materials is shown below.

Geotextile · Butyl liner · Rigid liner · Rigid cascade liner · Plastic sump · Artificial stone paver · Flat stone, irregular shape · Rock · Cobblestones · Brick · Sleeper (tie) · Log ring · Rustic post · Useful timber (wood) sections · Clear plastic pipe · Copper pipe · Copper-pipe joint · Armoured pipe · Plastic pipe · Plastic-pipe joint · Cement · Soft sand · Ballast · Gravel · Bark chips

TOOLS

Tools can be obtained from dedicated tool shops, DIY stores, builder's merchants and tool-hire (rental) companies. A selection of essential tools is shown below.

Tape measure · Pegs and string · Spirit (carpenter's) level · Garden rake · Trowel · Wheelbarrow · Gloves · Bucket · Spade · Shovel · Fork · Sledgehammer · Club (stonemason's) hammer · Bolster (brick) chisel · Bricklayer's trowel · Jig saw · Claw (brick) hammer · General-purpose saw · Knife · Electric (power) drill · Cordless driver · Twist, masonry and flat drill bits · Scissors

CONCRETE AND MORTAR

Concrete ~ Concrete is mainly used in foundations. Combine 1 part of cement, 5 parts of ballast (ballast is sand and gravel mixed together) and water to make a stiff mixture.

Mortar ~ Mortar is used in brick, block and stone walls. Combine 1 part of cement, 3 parts of soft (or 'builder's') sand and water to make a smooth mixture.

SAFETY WHILE YOU WORK

Always follow the manufacturer's instructions when using tools and materials. Work carefully and slowly and wear the appropriate protective gear as advised. Avoid working if you are tired or feeling unwell. Cement is corrosive, so wear goggles, a dust mask and gloves to protect yourself. Keep children away from work areas.

Oxygenation and filtration

Why are these necessary?

Filtered water has been pumped through a mesh to remove any algae and other unwanted detritus, while oxygenated water has either been bubbled through a fountain, or over a fall, or is water that contains plants that naturally give off oxygen. Although fish need good-quality, well-oxygenated water, this does not necessarily mean that it has to be clear. It is nice when you can see the fish, but some prefer to hide in murky, green-brown water.

When do I need oxygenation?

Oxygen is best thought of as a key that sets the whole ecosystem of the pond into operation. The oxygen passes through the water, the various life forms are then able to thrive and survive, the plants benefit, and so the wheel goes round. You particularly need oxygenation if the water looks green and scummy and/or the fish are dying or gasping for air.

When do I need filtration?

If you want the pond to have clear water, and yet you do not want plants – or at least not too many plants – then you need a filtration system. There are two types: a mechanical system that strains out solids, and a biological system that breaks down waste products. If you want perfectly clear water, you can go one step further and fit an ultraviolet (UV) radiation filter that collects and strains algae.

OXYGENATING PLANTS

To achieve healthy, good-quality water and encourage wildlife, it is a good idea to stock the pond with aquatic or submerged oxygenating plants. These are called oxygenators because they absorb carbon dioxide and give off oxygen – perfect for fish and other pond wildlife. If you look very closely at some of the hairier water plants, you will actually be able to see little bubbles of oxygen caught up in the fine fronds.

Ceratophyllum demersum (*Hornwort*) is a good choice for deep water.

Potamogeton crispus (*Curled Pondweed*) prefers still water and shade.

Ranunculus aquatilis (*Water Crowsfoot*), a small aquatic or submersible plant that shows its flowers just above the water, is a good oxygenator for a large wildlife pond.

FOUNTAIN

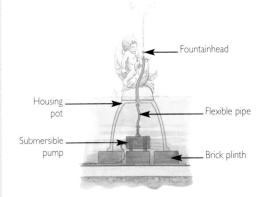

Fountainhead

Housing pot

Flexible pipe

Submersible pump

Brick plinth

Moving water tends to be healthy water. The action of a fountain, as the water bubbles and jets through the air, is enough to increase the oxygen content of the water significantly. The finer the spray, the higher the oxygen level. A fountain is a good, swift, low-cost option that can be up and running in the space of an afternoon. There are lots of fountain options on the market – everything from small self-contained pump-and-spray units, which come with their own integral filter systems, to huge statuary items that need a separate good-sized pump.

WATERFALL

Whereas a waterfall acts in much the same way as a fountain, in that the thin spread of water as it splashes and gushes over the fall gathers up oxygen, the set-up requires not only a larger pump than say a fountain but also the construction of a sump and a fall. A good option is to have the pump in a pond, so that the pond becomes the sump, and then to pump the water up to the top of a mound at the side of the pond, where it can gush out to run over one or more stone steps, and then flow back into the pond.

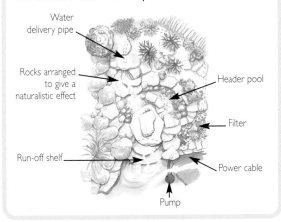

Water delivery pipe

Rocks arranged to give a naturalistic effect

Header pool

Filter

Run-off shelf

Power cable

Pump

FILTRATION

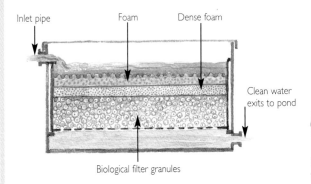

Inlet pipe

Foam

Dense foam

Clean water exits to pond

Biological filter granules

Separate filter

↗ Large, plantless ornamental pools and ponds require an external dual mechanical-biological filter system, complete with filters for the solids and a biological filter for water purification, with the whole system being contained within a tank. The water to be filtered is pumped out of the pond into the tank, where it flows down through various grades of foam that filter out the solids, and on through granules that encourage positive bacteria; the clean water then flows on out and back into the pond. The larger the pond, the bigger will be the system required.

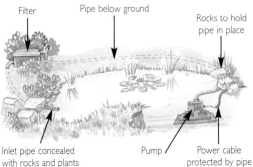

Filter

Pipe below ground

Rocks to hold pipe in place

Inlet pipe concealed with rocks and plants

Pump

Power cable protected by pipe

Pond pump and filter

↗ Large ornamental ponds – with few plants and no fish – require an external mechanical-biological filter. The set-up involves having a pump in the water and the filter system on dry land. The water is pumped out of the pond and into the filter. Once inside the body of the filter, the water drains down through the various layers and back into the pond. If you can run the returning water over a fall or through a fountain, so much the better.

Water-garden mechanisms

What exactly are these?

In water gardens, mechanisms are all the vital 'backstage' components, such as sumps, pumps, canals, automatic top-ups and overflows, that allow all the features within the garden to work. For example, without a sump and a pump you cannot have a waterfall, stream, spouting mask, self-contained water feature, and so on. If you are going to create a successful water garden, you will need to know about the mechanisms that make it all possible.

PUMPS, CABLES AND PIPES

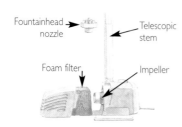

Fountainhead nozzle

Telescopic stem

Foam filter

Impeller

Pumps

↑ There are low-voltage submersible pumps to suit most water gardens. Before buying, decide how many litres (gallons) of water you want to move per minute or hour, and how far vertically you want to move it – in other words, what is the vertical distance from the surface to the top of the delivery pipe?

Cables and pipes

↓ There are two ways of getting water pipes and electric cables into the pond: you can pass them over the edge of the pond or water feature at some point that is hidden from view, or you can run a duct through a flange or gasket. The first option is easier.

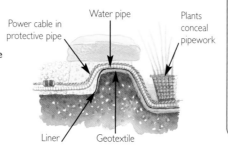

Power cable in protective pipe

Water pipe

Plants conceal pipework

Liner

Geotextile

Cleaning pumps and filters

Depending upon the size of pump and water quality, pumps and filters need frequent cleaning. The order of work is to turn off the power, unplug the electrics, lift the pump from the water, unclip the filter cover, and wash the whole thing in warm water. It is very important to make sure the electricity is switched off. Do not wash biological filters, other than as directed by the manufacturer.

PUMP INSTALLATION IN PONDS

To a great extent, the efficiency of any given pump – meaning the speed and quantity of the water flow – depends upon the distance the water has to travel. There are two options. You can have a direct installation or an indirect one.

Direct

Direct installation involves close-coupling the pump to the delivery end – so, for example, the water goes directly from the pump to the fountain, with there being only a few centimetres (inches) separating the two. This option wins on two counts: it is easy to install, and the friction between the pipe and the water is kept to a minimum.

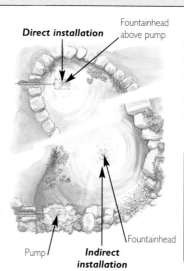

Direct installation

Fountainhead above pump

Pump

Indirect installation

Fountainhead

Indirect

Indirect installation involves having the pump and the delivery end remote from one another. For example, you might have the pump in the pond or sump, and the delivery end of the pipe several metres (yards) away at the other end of a stream. The greater the distance between the pump and the delivery end, the greater the loss in efficiency.

Sumps and reservoirs

A 'sump' is a purely functional, smallish container, usually hidden from view, full of water waiting to be pumped to another destination. A 'reservoir' serves much the same purpose, but tends to be larger and in some way decorative, and is on show.

SUMPS

A sump might be anything from a purpose-built brick box that has been cement-rendered and painted with waterproof paint through to just about any preformed plastic container that holds enough water. Many modern water features are based on simple pump-and-sump

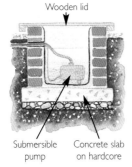

Wooden lid

Submersible pump

Concrete slab on hardcore

kits, with the sump, pump and fountain or other feature being designed and fitted all together. The water sits in the sump, the pump pushes the water up through say a fountain, the water drains back into the sump, and so on in a continuous cycle.

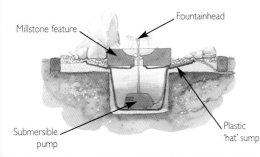

Millstone feature

Fountainhead

Submersible pump

Plastic 'hat' sump

WATERFALL RESERVOIR

A garden waterfall can be created by having two ponds, one much higher than the other. The lower pond is termed the reservoir, while the top pond is termed the header pool. In operation, the water is pumped from the reservoir, with the effect that the water in the header pool brims over in a single sheet to drop or fall directly down to the reservoir. The shape of the spillway or lip over which the water flows, and the size of the pump and the consequent rate of water flow, are the two features that decide the character of the waterfall.

Header pool

Spillway

Reservoir

Pump

Delivery pipe

RESERVOIRS

A good example of a reservoir is a small pond at one level that feeds a waterfall at a higher level (see 'Waterfall reservoir', top right). The small pond is a decorative, working pond, but at the same time it functions as a reservoir.

Natural spring reservoir A natural spring might be anything from a spout of water gushing from the ground – large enough to be a stream - through to a slow but steady seepage of water that results in a boggy area. To create a reservoir in a boggy area, dig a hole, and put a plastic container in the hole to prevent the sides collapsing in. The bigger the container, the larger the reservoir of water will be.

Rainwater reservoir The simplest way of creating a rainwater reservoir is to collect the rainwater from the roof – in a barrel butt, trough, tank or pond.

Canal reservoir A canal reservoir system can be created by building two split-level brick or block tanks, with a pump in the lower tank. In operation, the pump pushes water from the lower tank to the higher tank, with the effect that the top tank overflows into the lower tank, and so on.

TOP-UP SYSTEMS

Rainwater can be used for topping up ponds and streams. All you do is run underground pipes from the various downpipes around the house through to the pond you want to top up, and fit an overflow from the pond to a bog garden.

An automatic top-up system can be created by

Low wall defines edge of pond

Emergency water feed inlet pipe

Plastic liner pierced with occasional holes

Perforated hosepipe

fitting a water tank complete with a ballcock and main water feed in the ground at the side of the pond, so that the level of water in the tank is at the desired level within the pond. In operation, the falling and rising level of water within the pond opens and closes the feed valve in the tank.

NATURAL POND OVERFLOW

In the context of a natural pond, it is best to organize the overflow point so that surplus water is used to feed a bog garden. Just lower the rim of the pond slightly so that the excess water brims over into an area of bog planting. You could have rainwater from the roof being fed in from one side of the pond and the overflow dribbling out at the other.

Minimalist city water garden

Will this suit my lifestyle?

A minimalist water garden is clean and crisp, with white or pastel walls, white furniture and materials like copper, zinc, stainless steel and glass. The shallow water is crystal clear, and the plants are limited to grasses, palms and ferns. It is low-maintenance in that you don't have to mow lawns or prune trees, but you will have to keep the paintwork in good condition, polish the containers, and so on. A minimalist water garden always needs to look its best.

DESIGN OPTIONS

A design of this character will require a large pump for the waterfall.

A small sunken pond gives emphasis to the surrounding architectural planting.

A rill or canal, ending in a cascade onto pebbles, draws the eye and creates interest.

DESIGN COMPONENTS

If you look at minimalist garden designs in general, you will see that they are based on geometrical forms such as rectangles and cylinders, angles and smooth surfaces, with the man-made forms being offset by nature. This is an all-or-nothing style – you either go the whole hog or choose another style. Are you ready to opt for this distinctive look?

IS IT RIGHT FOR YOUR GARDEN?

This is not a garden for children or pets. It is a garden for adult entertaining and relaxing, meaning outdoor eating, reading and chatting. It needs to be tidy – no kids, dustbins (garbage cans) on view, brown earthenware flower pots, old deckchairs, or anything that will detract from the straight lines and smooth surfaces. Ask yourself whether this is going to work for you.

VARIATIONS TO CONSIDER

If you like this design but have a country site, you could put it in a high-walled area, so that you have a sophisticated minimalist water garden set within a natural garden. Such a juxtaposition of styles can look great.

Design guidelines for success

- Have high walls on the sides so that you can create a controlled environment.
- Render the walls – avoid having red brick and brown woodwork.
- Paint the walls flat white, or pastel colours such as blue and pale ochre.
- Build a round or square pond that is set flush with the paving.
- Use geometrical containers – white, glazed, zinc, glass or stainless steel – in cubes, cylinders and rectangles.
- Collect large, feature boulders, smooth and rounded to set off the geometrical forms.

MORE IDEAS FOR MINIMALIST CITY WATER GARDENS

A large man-made object such as this stone sphere is bound to invite comment, and looks good with restrained planting.

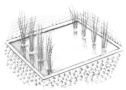

You can make a bold statement with straight-line planting – the plants have room to flourish but are controlled.

Although even the tiniest space can house a water garden, the smallness of the space demands quality details.

HOW TO CREATE A MINIMALIST CITY WATER GARDEN

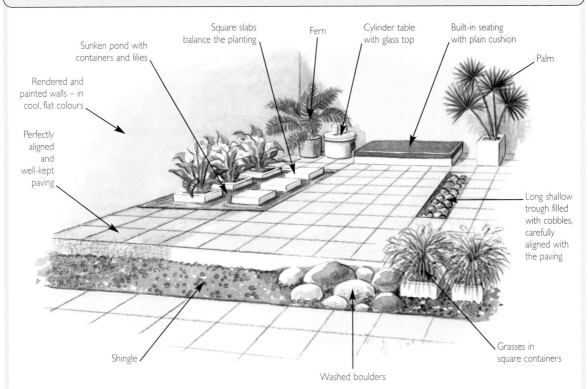

Sunken pond with containers and lilies

Square slabs balance the planting

Fern

Cylinder table with glass top

Built-in seating with plain cushion

Palm

Rendered and painted walls – in cool, flat colours

Perfectly aligned and well-kept paving

Long shallow trough filled with cobbles, carefully aligned with the paving

Shingle

Washed boulders

Grasses in square containers

If you have a city garden – best if it is walled – about 6 m (20 ft) wide and 15 m (50 ft) long, you can turn it into this minimalist water garden. If you like the design, but do not like the notion of digging, then consider having a raised pond with a decking surround.

Order of work

- Draw up your designs so that they take into account the house, the boundaries, immovable structures, drains and large trees.
- Give unwanted plants away or dispose of them.
- Render all the side walls.
- Build the pond.
- Fit a pump with a simple fountain spray.
- Paint the rendered walls white, pastel or another cool colour.
- Pave around the pond.
- Arrange carefully selected, washed boulders.
- Get as many containers as possible – white glass cubes and cylinders, metal boxes and so on (these must be 'cool' rather than traditional).

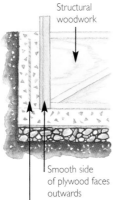

Structural woodwork

Smooth side of plywood faces outwards

Metal mesh for reinforcement

↑ *A cross-section detail showing the formwork needed for casting a pond with concrete sides.*

CARE AND MAINTENANCE

A minimalist garden needs, above all else, to be kept clean. If you see that there is a problem with litter or where to keep tools, you will need to build additional storage at the end of the season.

At the end and the beginning of each season, clean up dead leaves and remove damp mould. Renew paintwork.

The condition of the water relies on the pump and the filter system. Remove the pump and filter at regular intervals and clean all the moving parts. Pay particular attention to the filters – the bits that collect the rubbish.

Water the plants and check them for problems.

The furniture will need to be stored in a dry place during the winter months.

Development

You could add water features that bubble into or feed off the main pool. These could be in the form of self-contained features that are raised up and set on islands within the main pool. If you get fed up with the minimalist aspect of the design, you could increase the number of plants and introduce fish.

Willow-pattern water garden

The term 'willow pattern' describes the traditional blue-on-white chinoiserie design seen on both old and new earthenware pottery. The design features a legend that tells of a girl, her Mandarin father and a poor young man, ending with the couple finding eternal love as a pair of doves. The familiar images of a lake, pond or stream, pretty bridge, lattice-type fencing, apple blossom and willow trees make for a beautiful water garden.

DESIGN FEATURES

Doves
These symbolize eternal love

Willow tree
Stylized forms – a *Salix babylonica* (Weeping Willow) is a good option

Ornate bridge
Include a bridge or some statuary

Lattice fence
Basic square-form fence with diagonal cross-bracing

Apple blossom
The more blossom the better!

Pavilion
The details need to look oriental

Above: A small bridge is a great addition if you have the space, but can be difficult to incorporate in a small water garden.

Left: This is one version of the traditional willow pattern design found on pottery, showing all the required elements.

DESIGN COMPONENTS

The best way of understanding this design is to get yourself a willow-pattern plate, either from the 19th century or a modern one. If you look at the design, you will see that there are five primary components: a pavilion or summerhouse, the water, an ornate bridge, the trelliswork or rustic fencing, and the apple and willow trees – all with Chinese motifs.

IS IT RIGHT FOR YOUR GARDEN?

Of course, this design is more than a little bit kitsch – like something out of a Chinese-type pantomime – but the only way of doing it right is to get in there and enjoy the fun of it all. Right from the start you must uninhibitedly enjoy oriental imagery, and you must be romantic. Is this going to work for you?

VARIATIONS TO CONSIDER

If you like the design, but have not got the space for a pond, you could stay with the overall feel of the design, miss out the pond, and have a stream with a small header pool at one end and a sump and pump at the other.

Design guidelines for success

• Either have a large, natural-looking pond, with a stream running off it, or a meandering stream.

• Choose a summerhouse or gazebo that suits your needs, and create the look by fitting it out with oriental-style scrolls and motifs.

• Link the pavilion and the water with a small area of decking.

• Build a narrow bridge over the pond or stream.

• Decorate some part of the scene with latticework – either the fencing or the bridge.

• Choose Chinese containers.

• Plant apple trees, willows and bamboos.

• Have carp in the pond.

• Try to include a dovecote.

HOW TO CREATE A WILLOW-PATTERN WATER GARDEN

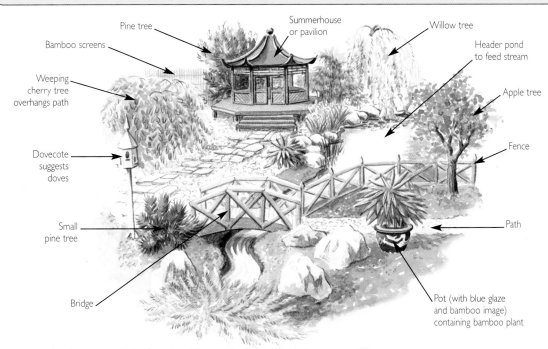

Pine tree
Bamboo screens
Weeping cherry tree overhangs path
Dovecote suggests doves
Small pine tree
Bridge
Summerhouse or pavilion
Willow tree
Header pond to feed stream
Apple tree
Fence
Path
Pot (with blue glaze and bamboo image) containing bamboo plant

You need to have a good-sized garden. The good news is that it is now possible to buy off-the-peg items that either are Chinese in origin or at least speak of China – bamboo plants, Chinese pottery, Victorian chinoiserie items such as ducks, screens and statuary, and so on.

Order of work
- Draw up your designs so that they take into account the house, the boundaries, immovable structures, drains and large trees.
- Give unwanted plants away or dispose of them.
- Fence the space with a mix of bamboo screens, hedges and willows.
- Build the pond with the stream running off it – have it meandering its way through the plot.
- Build the summerhouse complete with the decking.
- Build the bridge.
- Place rocks or slabs around the pond and along the stream.
- Get as many Chinese-type containers as possible – lots of blue, and Chinese brushwork designs.

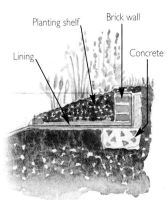

Planting shelf
Brick wall
Lining
Concrete

↗ *All the construction is hidden from view under a bank of earth.*

CARE AND MAINTENANCE

A natural-type pond and stream needs to be cleaned out at regular intervals.

In autumn, remove dead leaves and debris, trim back dying foliage, divide up plants and remove delicate plants for overwintering indoors.

In winter, take out dead leaves, remove and clean pumps and put a ball in the water to break up the ice.

In spring, clean out the pond, replace pumps, check the plants and replace if necessary.

The summerhouse needs to be checked before, during and after the winter to make sure that it is clean, dry and free from vermin.

Development

A project of this character can be good fun: you can furnish the summerhouse and the pond with boot- or garage-sale items; you can ask friends and family for bits and pieces that look Chinese; you can collect blue-and-white pottery for the summerhouse; you can have Chinese-themed food for the barbecue; and so on.

North American lakeside garden

Is a pier feasible?

Think about sitting quietly on the end of a wooden boardwalk pier jutting out over a lake, with the sun setting and no more than the plop of a leaping fish to break the silence. If this vision inspires you, start by visiting a nearby lake. Take note of any cabins, piers, jetties and boardwalks that may be there, as well as the type of plants and wildlife that inhabit the local area, and you will begin to get a vision of how your garden could be.

PIERS, DECKING AND BOARDWALKS

A peaceful pond with a beach and bank on one side, an area of planting and a wooden boardwalk leading to the water's edge.

A wooden deck perfectly complements a lakeside garden, and is the ideal spot for relaxing and watching any wildlife that may appear.

DESIGN COMPONENTS

In the design, you will see that, while there are six component parts – the pond, the decking pier, the Adirondack chair, the cabin, the water plants, and the trees all around – the focus of attention is on the small area in front of the cabin. The overall effect is one of stillness and calm – a natural lake in the country, lots of reeds and rushes, and fish. If you imagine an immense American or Canadian lake, and base your design on one little detail, you will have it about right.

IS IT RIGHT FOR YOUR GARDEN?

Although a large lake set in a big country garden would make the best setting for this, you can also create the effect with a small pond in a small garden – as long as you stay with the simplicity of the cabin and the decking, and as long as you cram the surrounds with a variety of trees and scrubby shrubs. Are you going to get all this into your available space?

Design guidelines for success

- Draw inspiration from North American folk images such as paintings and old photographs – perhaps travel photographs.
- Try for the largest possible pond.
- Build a simple cabin – nothing fancy or showy.
- Build a small area of decking in front of the cabin with the boardwalk pier branching off from the deck.
- Go for as many trees as possible – ones like *Salix* (Willows), *Acers* and *Malus sylvestris* (Crab Apple) – with climbers such as *Lonicera* (Honeysuckle) and *Humulus lupulus* 'Aureus' (Golden Hop). The plants need to look wild, lush and green.
- You must have plants that like damp and shade, such as hostas, ferns, irises and rushes, that are suitable for a bog garden.
- Search out a couple of simple rustic Adirondack-type chairs.

VARIATIONS TO CONSIDER

If you like the design but are short of space, you could have a small strip of decking jutting out over a pond, and then fit and theme existing items to suit. For example, you could modify the design so that an existing shed is at the centre of the design.

Decking set alongside a pond is a great place from which to enjoy the water.

HOW TO CREATE A NORTH AMERICAN LAKESIDE GARDEN

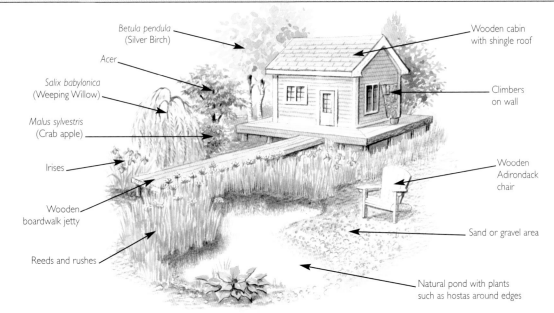

Betula pendula
(Silver Birch)

Acer

Salix babylonica
(Weeping Willow)

Malus sylvestris
(Crab apple)

Irises

Wooden
boardwalk jetty

Reeds and rushes

Wooden cabin
with shingle roof

Climbers
on wall

Wooden
Adirondack
chair

Sand or gravel area

Natural pond with plants
such as hostas around edges

For this look, you need a medium-sized garden to style or theme so that it resembles a lakeside fishing pier with trees, shrubs and bog gardens all around, with no flower beds or lawns anywhere in the design.

Wooden pile

Jetty

Concrete
foundation

↗ *Cross-section showing how the jetty is constructed with concrete foundations.*

Order of work

- Draw up your designs so that they take into account the house, the boundaries, immovable structures, drains and large trees.
- Give unwanted plants away or dispose of them.
- Fence the space with a mix of hedges and willows – and high wooden panels if you need to blank out neighbouring houses.
- Build a natural pond with a flexible liner, and create a natural edging.
- Use the offcuts from the pond liner to create the bog-garden hollows so that they are fed with the runoff water from the pond.
- Build the cabin complete with the decking.
- Cantilever a pier out from the decking so that it stretches out over the water.
- Plant the trees, shrubs, climbers and bog plants.

CARE AND MAINTENANCE

A natural-type pond needs to be cleaned out at regular intervals.

In autumn, remove dead leaves and debris, trim back dying foliage, divide up plants and remove delicate water plants for overwintering indoors.

In winter, take out dead leaves, and put a ball in the water to break up the ice so that the fish can breathe.

In spring, clean out the pond, check plants and replace if necessary.

The cabin needs to be checked before, during and after the winter to make sure that it's clean, dry and free from vermin.

The decking and pier must be scrubbed at regular intervals to stop them getting green and slippery.

Development

The best way to proceed with this project is to follow through and theme the entire garden. For example, you could decorate the cabin with a collection of fishing floats, duck decoys, or something that says more about the waterside atmosphere. You could go one step further and have bunk beds in the cabin – so that you or your kids can sleep out. It could be lots of fun. If you are worried about the children falling from the pier into the water, you could build a balustrade fence on it.

Japanese water garden

Although Japanese water gardens are perfect for small, enclosed spaces, simply because a good part of the Japanese tradition is concerned with smallness, privacy and quiet, they work just as well for a large, peaceful garden. Japanese gardeners have evolved a uniquely structured way of thinking about the pleasures of water and gardening, to the extent that they have formalized what is needed in the way of elements, features and plants.

A minimal H-spout and in-line delivery pipe positioned over a hewn-stone bowl make a fascinating Japanese-style feature.

DESIGN COMPONENTS

For this project, you need the biggest possible pool set within a quiet space, with a backdrop of plants like bamboos, *Acers* and dwarf pines. The other components are a stone lantern, boulders, rocks, summerhouse and a bamboo deer-scarer feature. You could also include a few stepping stones.

IS IT RIGHT FOR YOUR GARDEN?

Above all else, a Japanese water garden must be quiet and contemplative. It will not work if there are noisy children, plastic toys or boisterous pets. If you have a very large space, you could perhaps build a private garden within a garden, but it is not a good idea if you have children and a very small garden.

VARIATIONS TO CONSIDER

If you have a very small space – say a little yard – you can miss out the pool and have a water feature like a *tsukubai* stone basin full of water, or a *suiseki* stone basin. You can create the feeling and appearance of water by having raked sand, or a series of stepping stones going over a dry stream bed.

MORE IDEAS FOR A JAPANESE WATER GARDEN

A simple water basin with dribble-pipe feed and water dipper detail is effective.

A water basin and feed over a sunken echo chamber provides unusual sound.

A 'deer-scarer' consists of a block and pipe feed and a large striker stone.

A traditional Japanese stone lantern, which symbolizes light, fire and guidance.

Design guidelines for success

- Draw inspiration from an actual Japanese water garden you have seen in a film (movie), pictures or books.
- Enclose the space with high walls, bamboo screens or a belt of trees.
- Avoid painting wood with hot 'cedar'-type paints; use a thin wash of white emulsion (latex) to create a weather-worn effect.
- Use pines, willows and *Acers* as a backdrop.
- Include lots of mosses, ferns, grasses, dwarf pines and bamboos – but there must be no flower borders.
- Include a Japanese water feature such as a deer-scarer.
- Search out character stones that are worn and smooth.

HOW TO CREATE A JAPANESE WATER GARDEN

Salix babylonica
(Weeping Willow)

Pond

Deer-scarer

Bamboo
screening fence

Bamboo

Acer

Pinus (Pine)

Bamboos

Ferns

Island with
stone lantern

Irises

Grass or *Soleirolia soleirolii* (Baby's Tears)

Summerhouse
– a resting place
or bower

For this particular design, you will need a good-sized garden that you would like to turn into a peaceful Japanese water garden.

Order of work

- Draw up your designs so that they take into account the house, the boundaries, immovable structures and large trees.
- Put plants that you want to save on one side.
- Dig and build the largest possible pool. Use a butyl liner.
- Build a small island in the pool and set the stone lantern in place.
- Build a simple shelter.
- Put in one or more simple plank seats inside the shelter. Use old timbers.
- Plant bamboos and dwarf pines in containers. Plant *Soleirolia soleirolii* (Baby's Tears) to spread over the ground, and ferns and irises at the water's edge.
- Mulch the ground in and around the plants with crushed bark.

CARE AND MAINTENANCE

A Japanese water garden has been described as 'a slice of carefully controlled nature'. Everything needs to be carefully maintained, and yet it must look timeless, as if it has always been so.

The trick is to keep it clean and tidy without it looking overly manicured. Of course you need to weed, mow any grass, clean out the pool, and brush up dead leaves and so on, but do not overdo it.

If the grass goes mossy, fungi start growing on the fence and the grass or *Soleirolia soleirolii* (Baby's Tears) drape down into the pool at the water's edge, it will all add to the effect.

Development

You could introduce a few bonsai trees, perhaps set in a quiet corner. You could search out someone who is looking to get rid of things like moss, old stones, a fallen moss-covered tree, old oak beams and such like, and offer to take them off their hands.

You could extend the design to include an area of raked gravel, or perhaps a small enclosed sitting area.

Classical water garden

What makes a garden classical?

Aclassical water garden contains objects, items and images that draw inspiration, directly or indirectly, from ancient Greece and Rome. When you see water gardens in the grounds of grand houses, with symmetrical spaces either side of central walks, colonnades and fluted pillars, pergolas, formal ponds with nymph, god and dryad statuary and wall-mask water fountains, you are looking at objects and images influenced by classical designs and forms.

PERFECT SYMMETRY

A long canal pond set within a brick patio draws the eye down the length of the garden. The urn provides an extra touch of classicism.

A classical split-level pond with a wall-spout feed. The water gushes from the spout into the pond and on into the reservoir.

DESIGN COMPONENTS

With the pond sitting on the centre line, everything must be mirror-imaged and symmetrical to the pond. All the details – urns, containers, statuary, pergolas, the shape of the borders – must relate to ancient Greece and Rome.

IS IT RIGHT FOR YOUR GARDEN?

Above all else, a classical water garden is organized so that everything is centred on the pond, with the main viewpoint looking up or down the centre line. Ideally, you need a site that slopes slightly up or down from the back of the house, so that when you walk out of the house onto a patio you can instantly centre yourself on the pond and look out onto the symmetrical arrangement. Is this going to work for your site?

Design guidelines for success

- Draw inspiration from classical gardens in grand country houses – from photos, magazines, and travel brochures that show 18th- and 19th-century gardens in countries like England, France, Spain and Italy.

- Ideally, the site needs to be enclosed with high walls or high clipped hedges.

- Decide on the main viewpoint – say a patio at the back of the house – and have the centre line running off from this point.

- All the features – items, flower beds and so on – must be mirror-imaged along the centre line.

- Use *Buxus* (Box) hedges, *Cupressus sempervirens* (Italian Cypress), *Laurus nobilis* (Bay) in containers, *Taxus baccata* (Yew) and standard roses.

- Include areas of lawn inset with geometrical flower borders.

- Search out classical imagery such as fluted columns, Greek- and Roman-type statuary, and urns.

VARIATIONS TO CONSIDER

If you have a completely level site, you might have to move the earth so as to rearrange the levels. If the slope runs across the width of the garden, you could site the viewing patio away from the house, on the lower side.

MORE IDEAS

Fluted pillars can set the scene by evoking images of ancient Greece or Rome.

A stone bench with classical Greek or Roman details will enhance the effect.

HOW TO CREATE A CLASSICAL WATER GARDEN

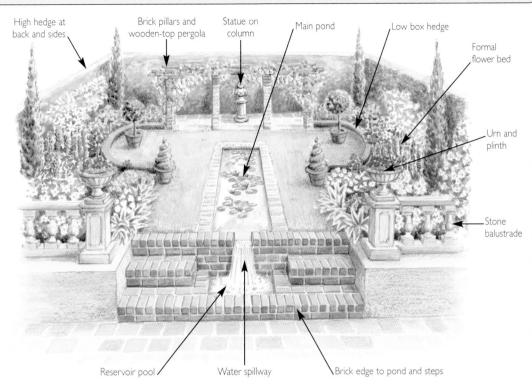

High hedge at back and sides

Brick pillars and wooden-top pergola

Statue on column

Main pond

Low box hedge

Formal flower bed

Urn and plinth

Stone balustrade

Reservoir pool

Water spillway

Brick edge to pond and steps

For this design, you need a good-sized garden sloping slightly up from the back of the house.

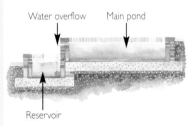

Water overflow

Main pond

Reservoir

↗ *Split-level pond of two brick pools. The water is pumped back to the main pool.*

Order of work

- Draw up your designs so that they take into account the house, the boundaries, immovable structures and large trees.
- Put plants that you want to save on one side.
- Run a centre line from the main viewpoint.
- Use bricks and a butyl liner to build a raised, split-level pond on the centre line.
- Fit the pump and filter in the lower level with the delivery pipe running up to the upper level.

- Build a red-brick or slab patio at each end of the pond, one on the lower level next to the house, and the other at the end of the garden.
- Build the steps leading up from the lower patio.
- Build a brick and wood pergola over the upper patio so that it is centred on the pond.
- Create lawns and flower beds.
- Position features such as statuary, urns and pillars, and arrange pieces of furniture on one or both of the levels.

CARE AND MAINTENANCE

A classical water garden must be clean, tidy and manicured.

The pump and filter must be cleaned at regular intervals – every week if there are trees shedding leaves into the water. Make sure that the spillway is clean and free from debris.

Trim fast-growing hedges little and often throughout the growing season. Trim edges of lawns.

The garden needs to look as if it belongs to ancient Greece or Rome, so remove everything that detracts from that image, such as children's toys and plastic pots.

Development

You could search out salvaged Victorian items such as stone or marble scrolls, stone-slab seats, broken columns – anything that looks as if it has just fallen off the back of an ancient Greek or Roman chariot. You could trim the box and/or the cypress so as to create topiary forms – pillars, cones, balls and prisms. You could build secondary water features like a classic wall mask spouting water.

Mountain-stream garden

Is a stream hard to create?

Visit a mountain stream, either physically or in your imagination. Take note of all the characteristic features – the way the water gurgles, ripples and rushes as it runs around rocks and flows over shallows, the deep, dark pools on the tight curves, the water-washed pebbles. Then go home to your garden and attempt to recreate some part of what you have seen. If you get even a fragment of it right, you will have a beautiful natural water garden.

NATURAL-LOOKING STREAMS

Above: A natural-looking, fast-running stream can be created on a base made up of sand, shingle and layers of rock.

Left: The perfect mountain stream. The bare rocks suggest that the stream might become a torrent during times of high rainfall.

DESIGN COMPONENTS

A mountain stream must be rocky, with lots of water gushing and rushing over stones, rocks and falls. The water must be fierce, fast-flowing and urgent. The bed of the stream needs to show lots of water-washed stones and shingle – with few plants in the actual water. There should be plenty of space, so that the viewer can stand back to take in the whole scene.

IS IT RIGHT FOR YOUR GARDEN?

Ideally, this project needs a large, long, rocky, sloping site in the country. The cost of transporting stone can be enormous, so it is good if you have a source of stone close by, but otherwise this project needs thinking about. As for building this project in a small, level town garden, it would not be easy.

VARIATIONS TO CONSIDER

If you have a level site in town, then either build the stream in miniature, or build a small fragment – just a bend and a single fall. You could have a good rush of water running swiftly in and out of the garden, perhaps from under a decking to run back into the ground, so as to fool the viewer into thinking that there is a fierce body of water gushing from a subterranean river.

Design guidelines for success

- Draw inspiration from an existing mountain stream.

- Either choose or build a sloping site.

- Bring in a good selection of stone – slices and slabs, plus water-washed boulders and shingle. Try to have one or two monolithic pieces.

- As the overall effect hinges on there being a lot of fast-flowing water, you need the biggest water pump that you can afford.

- There needs to be a header pool at the top end of the stream and a pump in a sump at the other.

- Keep most of the plants out of the water so as to create the feeling that the bed of the stream is subject to fast-flooding flows of water.

HOW TO CREATE A MOUNTAIN-STREAM GARDEN

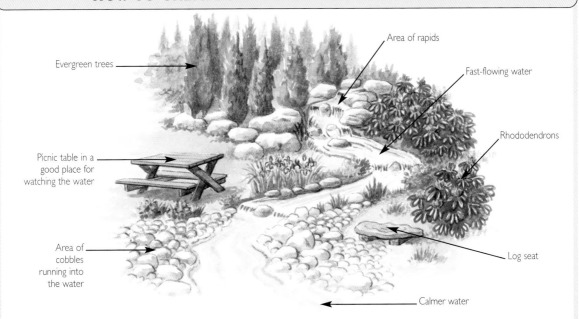

Evergreen trees

Area of rapids

Fast-flowing water

Rhododendrons

Picnic table in a good place for watching the water

Area of cobbles running into the water

Log seat

Calmer water

You need to have a plot that is about 30 m (100 ft) wide and 60 m (200 ft) long, ideally on a gentle slope, if you want to create this fast-flowing, rocky stream with several falls in level along the way.

Order of work

- Draw up your designs so that they take into account the house, the boundaries, immovable structures, drains and large trees.
- Give unwanted plants away or dispose of them.
- Mark out the route and excavate a series of wide, linked, U-section trenches.
- Dig a sump hole at the low end of the stream.
- Grade the trenches so that they drop one into another.
- Edge the excavation with a low brick or block wall.
- Cover the excavations with a layer of geotextile followed by a butyl liner.
- Set rocks and stones on pads of textile so that they are hard against the bricks.

- Bury a water-delivery pipe that runs from the sump pool to the top end of the stream.
- Fit the pump in the sump.
- Dress the whole stream with lumps of rock so that the bricks are completely hidden from view.
- Sculpt the earth so that it meets the rocks.
- Plant the edges on the side of the slow bend with plants like Japanese irises, grasses, *Osmunda regalis* (Regal Fern) and willows. As a backdrop to the scene, plant evergreen trees and shrubs of your choosing.

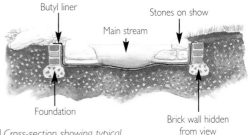

Butyl liner

Main stream

Stones on show

Foundation

Brick wall hidden from view

↗ *Cross-section showing typical construction for a mountain stream.*

CARE AND MAINTENANCE

As the whole character of this garden depends on there being a relatively large body of water either actually rushing down the whole length of the stream, or at least gushing in and out of the stream at some point, it is most important that the pump is kept in good working order.

Remove leaves, debris, rubbish and mud from the sump, and make sure that both ends of the water pipe are clear.

Remove and clean the pump at regular intervals.

Top the sump up if the water level drops.

Development

You could enlarge on the theme by running secondary streams into the main body of water. This would involve having more than one pump in the sump hole. You could run underground pipes from the rainwater downpipes, so as to save using domestic water. You could gradually build the whole garden up with pools, rocks and rockeries, creating a total scene like a slice from a mountainside.

Mediterranean water garden

What are the main features?

This style draws its inspiration from countries that fringe the Mediterranean sea. There are raised pools with tiled and coloured brick surrounds that look slightly Moorish or North African, pools and rills in enclosed, tile-decorated courtyards that look Moroccan or Spanish, clear pools set within white walls that look a little Greek, and so on. It is crisp, clean, hot and colourful, with lots of smooth rendered and mosaic-tiled walls, bright colours and clear pools.

WALLS, ARCHES AND TILES

A small raised pool with coloured tiles adorning its sides has a Spanish feel.

The shape and style of the arch suggests a Moorish or North African garden.

The tile-topped wall and the olive jar in this garden point to a Greek setting.

DESIGN COMPONENTS

If you look at a few examples of Mediterranean water gardens, you will see that characteristically they have a patio, high walls, pools of water and mosaics. While this design is essentially a split-level patio with a spout running water into a long rill at the lower level, you could create much the same effect by having an arrangement of pools on a single level.

IS IT RIGHT FOR YOUR GARDEN?

Ideally, for this to work you need to have a small courtyard garden with high walls all around it. If your garden is stark and unfenced, you will need to build high, rendered walls. Is this going to be possible with your garden?

Stand back and look at your garden. You have two choices if you live in the country and have a large, sprawling garden – you can build a complete courtyard with high walls all around it, or just build a patio in the appropriate amount of space, incorporating the rill.

Design guidelines for success

- Mediterranean water gardens are best built in courtyards, or at least in small, enclosed areas within a larger space.

- Ring the site around with high walls so that you can create a totally considered environment.

- Build rills and tanks out of bricks – they are much easier to handle than concrete blocks.

- Draw inspiration from classic Moorish gardens.

- Create mosaics using glass or ceramic tiles and broken crockery.

- Choose colours to complement the tiles.

- Go for exotic trees and plants – palms or palm-like trees, and grasses. Choose plants that like dry, sunny, sandy conditions (such as *Carex flagellifera, Selliera radicans, Festuca novae-zelandiae* and *Dracaena draco*).

VARIATIONS TO CONSIDER

If you were to look at the design in plan view, you would see that it is symmetrically centred on the rill. You could reduce or extend this arrangement to suit the size and shape of your garden. You could have smooth-curved shapes that echo the work of Antonio Gaudi – like the cathedral in Barcelona.

MORE IDEAS

Pieces of broken china and tiles can be used to create an exotic mosaic that will look wonderful in a Moorish garden.

The colours of these tiles suggest the bright sunshine, rich red and brown earth, foliage and pretty white houses of the Mediterranean.

HOW TO CREATE A MEDITERRANEAN WATER GARDEN

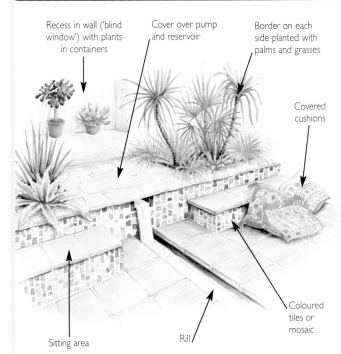

Recess in wall ('blind window') with plants in containers

Cover over pump and reservoir

Border on each side planted with palms and grasses

Covered cushions

Coloured tiles or mosaic

Rill

Sitting area

For this design, you need to have a plot that is about 15 m (50 ft) square, in which there is room to create a split-level water garden with steps linking the two levels.

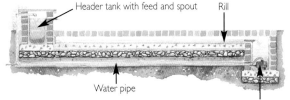

Header tank with feed and spout

Rill

Water pipe

Sump with pump

↗ *Cross-section of the rill, showing the best arrangement of the sump, pump and pipes.*

Order of work

- Draw up your designs so that they take into account the house, the boundaries, immovable structures, drains and large trees.
- Give any unwanted plants away or dispose of them.
- Build smooth-rendered block walls all around the site, or render existing walls.
- Build the pattern of low walls that divide the two levels, and define the various steps and planting areas.
- Dig a hole out for the pond and throw the earth up to the higher level.
- Set the rigid liner in place and sort out the shallow liner in the upper level. Link the two with a chute or spout of your choice – lead, copper, tile.
- Spread rubble to build up both the top and bottom levels and the steps. Compact the rubble so as to fill all voids.
- Set all the paving slabs in place.
- Tile or mosaic all vertical faces.
- Install a pump and filter so that the water will be pumped from the lower pool to the upper chamber.
- Plant exotic plants in and around the site (such as *Carex flagellifera*, *Selliera radicans*, *Festuca novae-zelandiae*, *Dracaena draco*, grasses, agaves, *Trachycarpus fortunei* (Chusan Palm) and *Cordyline australis*.
- Plant frost-tender plants in containers.
- Plant water plants such as *Glyceria maxima* var. *variegata* (Sweet Grass), *Acorus calamus* 'Variegatus' (Variegated Sweet Flag) and *Calla palustris* (Bog Arum) if there is space in the lower pool (not shown here).
- Cover the earth with a mulch of crushed stone, or crushed and rolled coloured glass.

CARE AND MAINTENANCE

Clean the paving slabs and the tiles or mosaics at regular intervals throughout the season. The mosaics are designed to be an eye-catching feature, so spend time making sure that they stay in good condition. Make repairs as soon as you spot a problem.

Remove leaves and debris from the pool.

Bring frost-tender plants in for the winter.

Check and clean the pump at regular intervals. The best way of cleaning a low-voltage pump is to strip it down and use washing-up liquid to clean off the algae. Never oil an in-pool pump – the oil could kill the plants.

Depending on the depth of your pool and the extent of your planting, you might have to divide the plants up at the end of the season.

Development

You could continue the theme by making a collection of pottery items. If you look at the work of Antonio Gaudi, the famous Spanish architect and artist, you will see that he created vast mosaics using broken crockery – plates, saucers, tiles, cups, indeed anything that had the right colours. You could try to decorate the backdrop walls with Gaudi-like motifs.

Castaway island garden

The story of the castaway *Robinson Crusoe*, written by Daniel Defoe in the early 18th century, provides the main features of this exciting water garden – a simple hut with a palisade fence around it, tropical plants, a beach running down to the sea, sand, shells, boxes, barrels and ropes. You could thatch the hut, build home-made bunk beds and chairs, collect nautical bits and bobs … there are endless possibilities. Children will love this project!

Will it look authentic?

CABINS AND HIDEAWAYS

A steep cliffside garden complete with a Robinson Crusoe-type cabin.

The details that you include will all help to suggest the setting for the island.

The perfect place to sit and dream about that faraway tropical paradise island!

DESIGN COMPONENTS

The design of this whole project draws its inspiration from the story of *Robinson Crusoe*. You have a choice: you can have the hut with a beach-type pool in front of it, or you can have the hut with a pool and a stream around it. Whichever you choose, the three main elements of the design are hut, water and beach.

IS IT RIGHT FOR YOUR GARDEN?

To get it right, the slope down to the shallow pool needs to be covered in washed sand and fine shingle or pebbles – no mud or plants. The clarity of the water hinges on there being a good-sized pump with a sophisticated filter system. Considering that this is a clear paddling pool rather than a pond – and therefore really good for children of a certain age – ask yourself whether it is going to fit into your scheme of things.

VARIATIONS TO CONSIDER

If you want to really splash out and take the design further, you could build a large paddling pool complete with a beach – as in some seaside theme parks.

MORE IDEAS

A barrel with a water pump makes a good feature, since both items are reminiscent of life in the 18th and 19th centuries.

A 'pool-and-pearls' water feature such as this will inspire thoughts of an exotic tropical beach and turquoise sea.

Design guidelines for success

- You need a pond that snakes out to become a stream.

- You need a cabin that looks like it has been made from salvaged driftwood.

- Either build the cabin on a slight rise or raise it up on short stilts.

- Make sure that the area from the cabin down to the water looks like a beach, with lots of sand and shingle.

- Try to include a palisade made from rustic poles or bamboo fencing.

- Plant lots of trees as a backdrop to the cabin.

- Plant a few exotic trees and plants – palms or palm-like trees, and bamboos. Choose plants that like dry, sunny, sandy conditions.

- Make your own rustic furniture.

HOW TO CREATE A CASTAWAY ISLAND GARDEN

Thatched roof

Cabin on legs

Bamboos and palms

Exotic plants

Palisade of bamboo or rustic poles

Shingle and sand

Scrubby grass

Stream

Pond

Barrels and rustic furniture

You will need to have a medium-sized garden to theme so that it looks like a scene from *Robinson Crusoe*, with lots of sand to recreate the beach.

Order of work

- Draw up your designs so that they take into account the house, the boundaries, immovable structures, drains and large trees.
- Give unwanted plants away or dispose of them.
- Enclose the space with a palisade-type fence of rustic poles or bamboo, and high wooden panels if you need to block out neighbouring houses.
- Build a large, shallow pond with a flexible liner, with the edges of the liner hidden from view.
- Run a stream around, so that it partially encircles the cabin.
- Sculpt the whole area with fine shingle, pea gravel and washed sand.
- Install a pump and filter so that the water is pumped from a sump at the end of the stream up to the pool.
- Build the cabin on a mound that overlooks the pond, or raise the cabin on short legs or stilts.
- Plant small areas of scrubby grass around the cabin.
- Plant exotic plants like bamboos, grasses, agaves, Chusan palm, *Dracaena draco* and *Cordyline australis* – anything that looks as if it belongs on a tropical island. Plant frost-tender plants in containers.

CARE AND MAINTENANCE

With the whole effect depending upon the water being clear, you have to make sure that the pump and filter are always in good working condition.

If you want to keep the pond clear – no fish – then every now and again throw a handful of salt into the water.

Remove leaves and debris and make sure that earth is kept back from the pool.

Bring frost-tender plants in for the winter.

Keep adding sand and shingle to the area around the cabin.

Give the cabin and fences a very thin wash of matt white paint so that it looks sun-bleached and weather-worn.

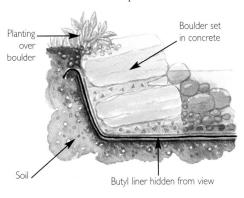

Planting over boulder

Boulder set in concrete

Soil

Butyl liner hidden from view

← *Cross-section of stream showing liner and edging details.*

Development

You could theme the hut – thatch the roof, add bits of driftwood, add beachcombed items such as old rope, logs, bits of chain or old portholes. If you live near the sea, you could search out a damaged rowing boat. You could collect boot- or garage-sale items to furnish the hut – lamp, anchor, shell pictures – anything that speaks of the sea.

Victorian covered water garden

This is a rather formal type of courtyard water garden, one with a small raised pond, lots of bricks and stone pavers, raised beds and containers, and lots of lush green foliage plants such as ferns, ivies, palms and grasses, all housed under a glass or plastic roof. If you try to imagine a mix between a modern conservatory and a grand but somewhat fading foyer in a Victorian-Italian, palm-court type hotel, you will have just about the right idea.

COVERED COURTYARDS

A formal courtyard water garden topped with a pergola-type roof.

A conservatory with a vine-covered trellis acting as a roof, with cast-iron furniture.

The found columns and the painted trellis give this garden an old-fashioned look.

DESIGN COMPONENTS

There are five primary elements: the red-brick or stone paved patio, the simple formal raised pond, the roof (in this design a see-through one of glass or plastic), the plants in containers, and the columns. You could also have some high trellis screens at the sides. If you get it right, it will feel warm, sheltered, slightly grand and extremely private.

IS IT RIGHT FOR YOUR GARDEN?

This is the perfect design for a small, partially walled space, when you want to sit outside without worrying about the weather or being overlooked by the neighbours. The roof and trellis screens not only shelter you from wind, sun and rain but also ensure that all-important privacy.

Design guidelines for success

• Draw inspiration from photos, magazines and historical accounts – anything that tells you more about mid- to late 19th-century covered water gardens.

• Ideally, the site needs to be partially enclosed with high walls or fences at the sides.

• This design can be modified so that it works just about anywhere – in a small courtyard garden in the city, in an enclosed area in a large country garden or even in a large conservatory.

• There needs to be a small, raised, formal pond, round or square.

• There could be a very small fountain in the pond.

• The area around the pond must be paved with bricks and/or stone slabs.

• The area must be covered with a glass or plastic roof.

• There needs to be a pump and filter in the pond to keep the water in good condition.

VARIATIONS TO CONSIDER

You could achieve much the same feeling by building the pond in a large conservatory. You could miss out the columns and trellis, and have a good-sized conservatory with a glass or plastic-sheet roof covering the whole water garden area.

MORE IDEAS

Real fossils look good, and help to suggest that the garden has Victorian origins.

The shape and style of the statuary that you choose to put in the garden will form the key to the whole design.

HOW TO CREATE A VICTORIAN COVERED WATER GARDEN

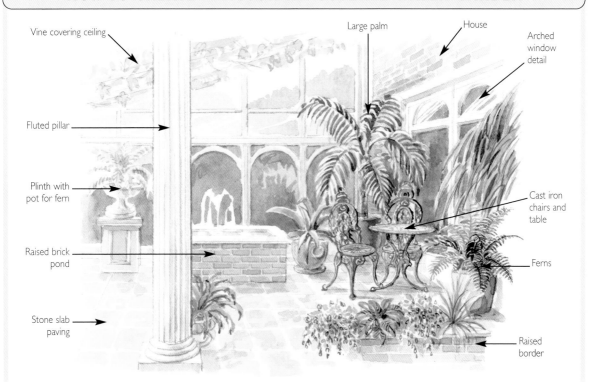

Vine covering ceiling

Large palm

House

Arched window detail

Fluted pillar

Plinth with pot for fern

Cast iron chairs and table

Raised brick pond

Ferns

Stone slab paving

Raised border

You need a relatively small space, about 6 m (20 ft) square, that you would like to turn into a covered water garden.

Order of work

- Draw up your designs so that they take into account the house, the boundaries, immovable structures and large trees.
- Put plants that you want to save on one side.
- Build the pond with a rigid plastic liner.
- Build a level patio area around the pond; use red bricks and/or stone slabs.
- Cover the area with a plastic-sheet or glass roof, complete with fancy columns.
- Add containers planted with old-fashioned plants like hostas, ferns, ivies, fuchsias and lilies.
- Plant grapevines at the sides.

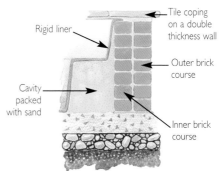

Rigid liner

Tile coping on a double thickness wall

Outer brick course

Cavity packed with sand

Inner brick course

↗ *Cross-section of a raised brick pond showing a rigid liner set on a foundation of hardcore (rubble) and concrete, with sand between wall and liner.*

CARE AND MAINTENANCE

A traditional covered water garden looks its best when there is Victorian-type cast-iron furniture and lots of plants, so that the whole area looks nicely cluttered. You may think this means that you can just sit back and let the mess pile up, but it needs to be carefully managed and contrived.

There is a lot of cleaning and maintenance. The pond must be kept in good order. The pump and filter must be cleaned regularly, ideally every week. The patio must be free from debris and broken pots, your chosen cover of glass or plastic sheet must be kept clean, and so on.

Development

You could search out salvaged Victorian or Edwardian items, such as Minton tiles, portrait busts, cast-iron lamps, ethnic brass and ironwork – anything that helps to create a nicely rich and faded feeling. You could build secondary water features like a classic mask spouting water. You could also have a small fountain bubbling away in the pond.

Wildlife water garden

How can I attract wildlife to the pond?

All you need is a natural-looking pond, a bog garden around some part of the pond, trees, nesting-boxes and pole-houses, piles of mossy logs and leaf litter, and a carefully considered mix of just the right plants, and nature will do the rest. It gets really interesting, though, especially for children, when small birds start eating the bugs, and reptiles and amphibians come in, attracting bigger birds and mammals, and so on, until you have a whole living ecosystem.

NATURALLY ATTRACTIVE

A good wildlife water garden is going to attract fish-eating birds like this heron.

Be aware that a wildlife pond is an exciting but potentially dangerous place for toddlers.

Duck houses are fun, but remember that foxes can swim and may target the house.

DESIGN COMPONENTS

For maximum impact – to attract a broad range of animals – a good wildlife garden needs water, lots of ground cover, trees and all the decaying debris that such a scenario produces. A woodland-glade wildlife garden is a good option. The components are a small, level area of grass or woodchip, a pond, a meandering path, a place to sit, trees all around, and lots of decaying wood and leaves.

IS IT RIGHT FOR YOUR GARDEN?

By its very nature, a garden of this character will be shady with lots of wood and leaf debris underfoot. You will attract wildlife, but will you be happy with the gnats and the apparent uncared-for look? Will it be safe for your children or pets?

VARIATIONS TO CONSIDER

If you are not so keen on the woodland, you could have something like a meadow water garden. You would still attract wildlife, but fewer birds. You could miss out the grass and go for a thick mulch of woodchip or crushed bark instead.

MORE IDEAS

A treehouse is the ideal observation platform for watching birds and animals.

A nesting box designed for treecreepers is a good addition to a wooded site, and may also attract bats.

> ### Design guidelines for success
>
> • Although, ideally, you need a good-sized site – the bigger the better – it could be managed on a small plot of say 25 m (80 ft) square. A broad site is better than a narrow one.
>
> • You need a pond, and the bigger it is the better.
>
> • Include a bog garden at the side of the pond.
>
> • You need trees around the site, the more the better.
>
> • Fit bird houses and boxes in and under the trees.
>
> • Plant scrub trees and shrubs – species that are native to your area.
>
> • Spread a layer of woodchip, crushed bark or leaf litter over the ground.
>
> • Put piles of logs in various places throughout the site.

HOW TO CREATE A WILDLIFE WATER GARDEN

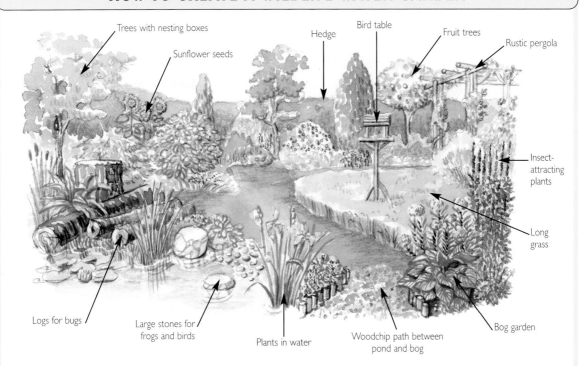

Trees with nesting boxes

Sunflower seeds

Hedge

Bird table

Fruit trees

Rustic pergola

Insect-attracting plants

Long grass

Logs for bugs

Large stones for frogs and birds

Plants in water

Woodchip path between pond and bog

Bog garden

To create a sort of forest-glade wildlife garden complete with a pond, you will need an area at least 25 m (80 ft) square.

Order of work

- Draw up your designs so that they take into account the house, the boundaries, immovable structures, drains and large trees.
- Give unwanted plants away or dispose of them.
- Dig out and build the pond. A butyl liner is the best option for a natural-looking pond.
- Use the offcuts of butyl to create one or more bog-garden areas.
- Plant the primary trees – species that grow wild in your area.
- Plant the pond with a full range of plants – bog plants like *Miscanthus sinensis* 'Zebrinus' (Striped Grass) and *Osmunda regalis* (Royal Fern), marginals like irises, *Glyceria maxima* (Sweet Grass), *Calla palustris* (Bog Arum) and *Acorus calamus* 'Variegatus' (Sweet Flag), floating plants like *Myriophyllum aquaticum* (Parrot's Feather) and *Azolla caroliniana* (Fairy Moss), submerged plants like *Ranunculus aquatilis* (Water Buttercup) and *Ceratophyllum* (Hornwort) and deep-water plants like *Nuphar japonica* (Japanese Pond Lily) and *Nymphoides peltata* (Fringed Water Lily).
- Underplant the trees with shrubs and ground cover.

CARE AND MAINTENANCE

The pond needs to be cleaned at the start and finish of the season – late winter and early spring. Remove leaves and debris from the pond and pile it up to rot.

Make sure that new trees are stable and not overwhelmed by a single species of weed.

Clean the bird boxes out in winter.

Make sure the paths are kept clear so that you can enjoy the garden and see the various bird boxes.

Development

You could build a small hut or hide, so that you can watch the wildlife without being seen yourself. You could also make the hide really comfortable so that you can enjoy long periods of quiet observation and meditation. You could build small underground boxes for animals like badgers, rabbits, mice and snakes.

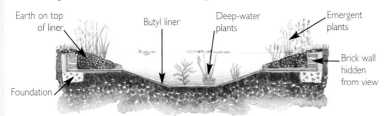

Earth on top of liner

Butyl liner

Deep-water plants

Emergent plants

Brick wall hidden from view

Foundation

↗ *Cross-section showing the elements and construction of a 'natural' pond.*

Meadow-stream garden

What are the main features?

Most natural meadow streams are slow-running and twisty, with wild grasses and a variety of flowers growing at the sides; part of the stream is usually overhung with water-loving trees such as willows. The ditch is shallow, with little or no fall along its length. The whole area alongside the stream is damp and soft. If you like tadpoles, frogs, newts and bog gardens, and wish to create a calm, low-key water garden, this project will suit you well.

NATURAL INFORMALITY

A ditch running into a stream results in moving water, providing sound and action.

Meadow streams are characterized by muddy shallows and rampant plant growth.

In a large garden, a meadow stream can be combined with a wildlife pond (see page 32).

DESIGN COMPONENTS

This design needs five primary components: a wild meadow, a meandering stream, a grassy bank or two at some point along the stream, a few willow trees, and of course the characteristic meadow planting.

IS IT RIGHT FOR YOUR GARDEN?

In terms of the meandering shape, this design will work in quite a small space, but the site needs ideally to be moist and more or less level. Meadow-stream plants need year-round damp conditions. Is your garden going to meet these needs?

VARIATIONS TO CONSIDER

If your garden is steep, you can either go for the mountain-stream design (see page 24), or you could modify this design so that you have a sort of mountain stream which levels out to become a meadow stream.

MORE IDEAS

Natural items can make wonderful sculptures for the garden. You could start a collection of rocks, boulders, fossils, driftwood, fallen branches, and such like.

Stepping stones work beautifully in a shallow stream. Use naturally flat-topped local stones, and try to position them to suit the location.

Design guidelines for success

• Ideally the site needs to be level.

• The shallow ditch through which the stream will flow needs to twist and turn throughout the site, so that the loops and turns form partially enclosed mounds.

• The margins of the stream should be planted with meadow-stream plants such as irises and rushes.

• Some areas beside the stream can be made into bog gardens.

• There needs to be a good number of *Salix* trees (Willow).

HOW TO CREATE A MEADOW-STREAM GARDEN

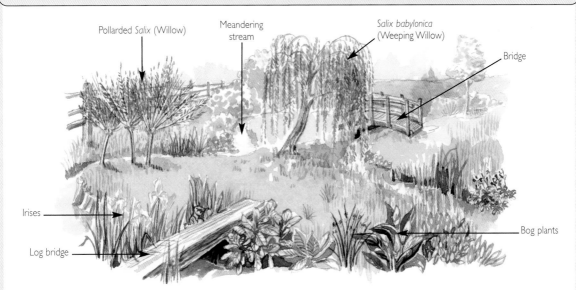

Pollarded *Salix* (Willow)

Meandering stream

Salix babylonica (Weeping Willow)

Bridge

Irises

Log bridge

Bog plants

You need a level, low-lying area about 15 m (50 ft) square in which to create a slow-flowing, meandering stream.

Order of work

- Mark out the route and excavate a continuous meandering V-section trench, about twice the width of the envisaged stream. Try to have the start and finish points close to each other.
- Dig a sump hole at the low end of the stream.
- Construct a pool at the top end of the stream so that the water will trickle over into the stream proper.
- Cover the excavation with a layer of geotextile, followed by butyl liner, and then more geotextile. You can use any scrap butyl to create bog gardens.

- Cover it all with a 10 cm (4 in) layer of concrete.
- Bury a water-delivery pipe that runs from the sump pool to the top end of the stream.
- Fit the pump in the sump.
- Sculpt the banks so that they are nicely curved, with high places to sit and low boggy areas to the side.
- Plant the edges of the slow bend with plants like Japanese irises, flowering and striped rushes, grasses, *Caltha palustris* (Marsh Marigold), *Myosotis scorpioides* (Water Forget-me-not) and *Osmunda regalis* (Regal Fern). As a backdrop to the whole scene, plant items like *Salix* spp. (Willows), *Hydrangea macrophylla* and other trees and shrubs that thrive in damp conditions.

CARE AND MAINTENANCE

Since the whole character of this garden depends on there being a relatively large body of water running slowly around the whole length of the stream, it is most important that the pump be kept in good working order.

Remove leaves, debris, rubbish and mud from the sump, and make sure that both ends of the water pipe are clear.

Remove and clean the pump at regular intervals.

Top the sump up if the water level drops.

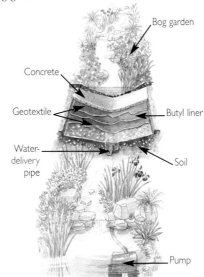

Bog garden

Concrete

Geotextile

Water-delivery pipe

Butyl liner

Soil

Pump

Development

You could enlarge on the theme by having a pond with extensive bog gardens – perhaps even a pond that sends water back into the stream. This would involve having more than one pump in the sump. You could top the stream up by having underground pipes running from the house rainwater downpipes.

You could gradually theme the whole garden with little bridges, wild meadow plants, small areas of lush grass and so on, to create a total scene resembling a slice from a water meadow.

◥ *Cross-section of a planted stream showing the sequence of layers needed.*

Covered patio water garden

Will it be safe?

This style is perfect if all you want is a large, level, covered area with just a touch of water to make it a little more dynamic. If you are worried about toddlers and water safety, choose a wall-hung mask feature that spouts water into a sink or trough. The children can have the fun of water play, and you can sit out on the patio and enjoy the sights and sounds of moving water. If your water garden has to be child-friendly, then a patio water garden is a good choice.

PATIO POSSIBILITIES

A free-standing, brick-built, wall-mask water feature is safe as well as attractive.

A small town garden can be easily turned into a charming covered patio water garden.

This one-time raised border has been transformed into an elegant water feature.

DESIGN COMPONENTS

This design focuses on just four components: the patio, the water feature, the containing wall or fence, and the cover that goes over it all. The idea is that you can enjoy the patio without giving a thought to the weather, and/or without worrying about the kids and the water.

IS IT RIGHT FOR YOUR GARDEN?

Because the design works for even the smallest garden, you need ask yourself only two questions: what are you going to use for the cover, and is the cover going to have a visual impact on the neighbours?

VARIATIONS TO CONSIDER

There are lots of cover options. You could have a rigid plastic roof on a pergola frame, or a striped canvas awning like a marquee, or a canvas awning that reefs in a bit like a roller-blind or a sail, or a permanent glass roof.

MORE IDEAS

Cross-section of a miniature pot fountain created using three ceramic pots.

A raised pond can be set into a corner of the patio, using a curved brick wall at the front.

Design guidelines for success

- You need an area that is as big as a large room.

- The patio needs to be paved with bricks, concrete slabs, stone pavers or whatever you prefer.

- The patio must be covered to keep off the rain.

- There needs to be a small water feature such as the child-friendly spouting head shown here, but you could use anything that fits into your scheme.

- The patio should be surrounded with something like raised beds or a picket fence, to keep the children in view.

HOW TO CREATE A COVERED PATIO WATER GARDEN

Clear, rigid roof on pergola frame

Ivy

Water feature using a stone urn

Trellis with climbing plants

Hanging baskets

Raised border with *Lavandula* (Lavender)

Steps to garden

Tender plants in pots

Fuchsias in raised border

You need a plot that is about 6 m (20 ft) square – either a courtyard or a small area within a much larger garden – to create this covered patio complete with a child-friendly water feature.

Order of work

- Draw up your designs so that they take into account the house, the boundaries, immovable structures, drains and large trees.
- Give unwanted plants away or dispose of them.
- Build the patio, complete with walls, fences or raised beds around it.
- Build the cover from canvas awning, rigid plastic sheet, glass or whatever waterproof material you choose.
- Build and fit the water feature complete with a pump and filter.
- Plant sweet-smelling plants in and around the edges or raised beds – a few *Ceanothus* (Californian Lilac), *Lavandula* (lavender), fuchsias, *Buddleja* and various grasses. Plant some frost-tender plants in containers.

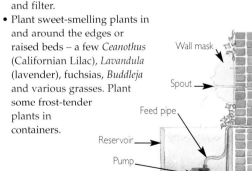

Wall mask

Spout

Feed pipe

Reservoir

Pump

↗ *Cross-section of a wall-mask water feature using a separate container such as a stone urn (see also page 39 for a similar feature).*

CARE AND MAINTENANCE

In the sense that a patio is a garden room, you must keep it clean and tidy just like any other room in the house. Leaves and debris have to be cleaned up, toys put away, furniture kept in good order and carefully arranged, and so on.

Make sure that all the water-play toys – cups, saucers, flexible tubes, water funnels, boats and such like – are made from unbreakable plastic. Do not let the children play with anything that could be dangerous, such as ceramic or glass, or anything that might get stuck in the pump, such as sand.

The cover – the canvas, plastic or glass – must be cleaned at regular intervals.

Make sure that the pump and filter are always in good working order.

Bring frost-tender plants and fragile furniture in for winter storage.

Development

If you enjoy eating and sitting out, you could extend the season by partially covering the patio in at the sides and by having lighting and heating. You could have a barbecue in a safe area close by. If there are lots of children's toys, you could build some sort of storage for them. If the cover is made from rigid plastic sheeting, you could attach slats both under and over it – so that it looks better, and the slats add a degree of shade. You could have climbing plants growing over it all.

Courtyard water garden

Is there room for a water garden?

Whatever the size of your courtyard, there will be room for a water garden. There might only be space for a small wall-mask water feature – perhaps no more than a terracotta mask spouting water into a stone or metal trough – but you will still be able to experience all the sights and sounds of water. Of course, if you grow some water-loving plants around the trough, in raised beds or containers, then you can create the illusion of size.

SMALL IS BEAUTIFUL

A small wall-mask water feature is a swift option, especially if you hang the mask from an existing wall and use a found container.

A group of water plants in containers, alongside a miniature container pond, is a good option for a very small courtyard.

A preformed liner set within a low brick wall makes a great raised pond, perfect for a medium-sized courtyard.

Walk around your courtyard and have a look at what exists. Are there well-built boundary walls that you could use as a backdrop to the main feature? Is there an outside water tap (faucet)? Is there an outside power supply? Is the ground made up of bricks, slabs, stone, concrete, flower beds or lawn?

IS IT RIGHT FOR YOUR GARDEN?

Will you be able to dig holes? Where would you put the earth? Do you have an access to the courtyard – other than through the house? Can you build directly onto say an existing patio base, or do you need to build foundations? Consider how the plans will affect the kids, neighbours and pets.

VARIATIONS TO CONSIDER

Is there space enough for a sunken pond? Or would you prefer a raised pond? Once you have decided on raised versus sunken for the pool, then you will have to think about the various design and material options. Do you prefer brick, stone or wood?

Design guidelines for success

- Try as far as possible to build all the existing structures into the design.
- Use traditional materials like brick, stone and wood – it is easier than using modern materials like glass, stainless steel and plastic.
- Make sure that the design of the water garden complements the design of your house.
- Draw inspiration from other interests, such as collecting nautical items like brass portholes, chains and ropes.
- Draw inspiration from your other gardening interests – container plants, the use of wooden decking, a collection of terracotta, a liking for climbing plants, and so on.

MORE IDEAS FOR A COURTYARD GARDEN

A 'seashore' fountain complete with beach finds – driftwood, shells, seaweed and shingle.

A bubbling fountain with a flow of water over a large, pre-drilled stone or ceramic ball.

A miniature millstone with a low bubble fountain that allows water to flow over the stone.

Ceramic, lead or bronze and stone-effect wall masks are available in many designs.

A cascading water feature in the form of an old pump handle and a series of half-barrels.

HOW TO CREATE A COURTYARD WATER GARDEN

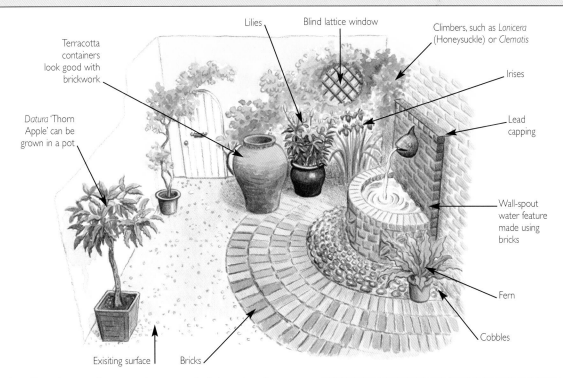

Lilies

Blind lattice window

Climbers, such as *Lonicera* (Honeysuckle) or *Clematis*

Terracotta containers look good with brickwork

Irises

Lead capping

Datura 'Thorn Apple' can be grown in a pot

Wall-spout water feature made using bricks

Fern

Cobbles

Exisiting surface

Bricks

A wall-mask water feature makes a wonderful courtyard centrepiece. This project is based on the premise that you have an existing courtyard. While this feature is designed to be entirely free-standing, you can modify it by hanging the mask from an existing wall and using a found trough (see page 37).

Order of work
• Repair existing courtyard walls or build new ones.
• Check that the patio is sound and build the trough.
• Position the ducting and build the backing wall.
• Render the inside of the trough with mortar.
• Fit the mask, pump and electrics.
• Dress the courtyard with container plants – lilies, grasses, ferns and irises – and climbers around the walls. Include a shrub such as *Datura* 'Thorn Apple' if there is room.

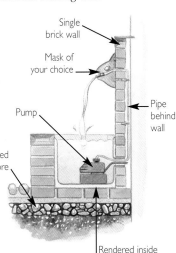

Single brick wall

Mask of your choice

Pump

Compacted hardcore

Pipe behind wall

Rendered inside

↗ *Cross-section of a brick-built wall-mask water spout (see page 37 for a similar feature).*

CARE AND MAINTENANCE

Spring cleaning Put the pumps in the pond and make sure they are in good working order. Replace tender plants.

Summer chores Clean the filters weekly. Skim off algae and debris. Keep the pond topped, and run the fountains to oxygenate the water.

Autumn care Remove dead foliage, divide vigorous plants and remove fallen leaves. Take frost-sensitive plants indoors.

Winter work Remove and clean pumps. Remove the remaining dead leaves. Put a ball in the water to create a breathing hole in the ice.

Development

One of the joys of gardens in general and water gardens in particular is the way that they swiftly evolve – plants grow, fish multiply, the surfaces break down and change colour, and so on. It is important that you are ready to modify the structures and planting to suit your changing needs.

Illuminated fountain garden

Is installing a fountain easy?

The sight and sound of water gushing up through a fountain is wonderfully exciting, but when you combine them with darkness and artificial lighting you have a truly magical mix. A small courtyard makes the perfect setting for a good-sized illuminated fountain. As for the technical difficulties of installing the fountain and the lighting, the introduction of low-cost, easy-to-fit, low-voltage systems has suddenly made it all possible for just about everyone.

LET THERE BE LIGHT

Modern Mediterranean garden with dramatic under-plant lighting.

Light coming from above (known as top lighting) gives a clear view.

The under-lit arch behind this water feature is used to create a striking effect.

DESIGN COMPONENTS

A garden of this character is made up from five components: the courtyard setting, a circular raised pond, a good-sized fountain, the artificial lighting, and the plants in raised beds or containers all around the edges.

IS IT RIGHT FOR YOUR GARDEN?

This is an ideal project if you have an existing small courtyard, but can be a very expensive option if you have to specially create a walled space.

Design guidelines for success

• You need a raised pond, preferably circular.

• You need a good-quality fountain – there are many options, including small fountains made from resin, statue fountains, fountains made from reconstituted stone, genuine old stone fountains from salvage yards, new fountains, and so on.

• You need a relatively small, private space with high walls all around it.

• You need lighting – ordinary exterior lights wired off from the house, and low-voltage garden lights designed specifically for underwater use.

• You need paving material of your choice, such as brick, new stone, salvaged stone or reconstituted stone.

• You need as many low-care plants as possible, such as ferns, grasses, clipped *Laurus nobilis* (Bay) trees and potted plants. Be aware that dark green foliage and lights go hand in hand.

VARIATIONS TO CONSIDER

If you have a large, open garden, you could build a courtyard (a sort of small room within a room), you could have the fountain on an open patio, you could have the fountain as a small detail in a much larger, classical garden, or you could create a sort of romantic, ruined garden that features a fountain at its centre.

MORE IDEAS

Candle lanterns are good fun, and are perfect if you want a low-cost form of lighting.

A modern globe light provides a traditional effect, rather like a Chinese lantern.

HOW TO CREATE AN ILLUMINATED FOUNTAIN GARDEN

Lights hidden under plants

Carefully placed lights add drama

Clipped *Laurus nobilis* (Bay) tree

Lights used to illuminate ground

Lights in pond

Sweet-smelling herbs in raised bed

You need a small, enclosed courtyard about 9 m (30 ft) square to create this garden.

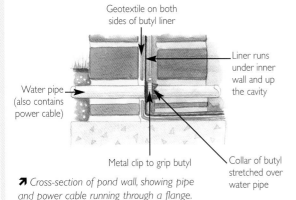

Geotextile on both sides of butyl liner

Liner runs under inner wall and up the cavity

Water pipe (also contains power cable)

Metal clip to grip butyl

Collar of butyl stretched over water pipe

↗ *Cross-section of pond wall, showing pipe and power cable running through a flange.*

Order of work

- Draw up your designs so that they take into account the house, the boundaries, immovable structures, drains and large trees.
- Give unwanted plants away or dispose of them.
- Build the circular pond using a flexible liner – with the ducting for the power cables running through the liner – with a flange to fit.
- Set the fountain up at the centre of the pond on a plinth made from a stack of paving slabs.
- Set your chosen underwater lighting up on a shelf within the pond.
- Pave the courtyard.
- Complete the planting around the edges, using architectural plants such as *Trachycarpus fortunei* (Chusan Palm), *Phormium tenax* (New Zealand Flax), *Buxus sempervirens* (Box) and *Laurus nobilis* (Bay), and sweet-smelling plants like lavender and other herbs.

CARE AND MAINTENANCE

You might think that a small courtyard is an easy-care option but, since the whole garden is centred on the fountain, raised pond and lighting, it is very important that it should all be clean, tidy and in good working order.

Sweep up leaves and debris, and clean the pond and the pump regularly.

Pay particular attention to the inside surface of the pond and the lighting units.

Make sure that all plugs, cables and connecting units are in good order.

Development

You could theme the courtyard with collected items, such as statuary, pots, wall-hung containers and old tiles. You could complement the fountain with a secondary water feature – perhaps a leaden, wall-mounted spouting mask (see pages 37 and 39). You could furnish the courtyard with old stone items such as seats, urns and busts.

Seaside garden

Visit your favourite stretch of seaside and decide what makes it so special. It might be a long stretch of sandy beach, with a community of brightly coloured wooden chalets with hand-painted names, all decked out with found items such as shells, driftwood, ropes, anchors and bits of old boat. Alternatively, it could be a bustling little port with piles of fishing nets and lobster pots lying around. Simply try to recreate your chosen theme in your garden.

BEACHCOMBING FOR IDEAS

Group all your collected items together for best effect, and to create a mood picture.

Draw inspiration from any real seaside gardens that you are able to visit.

You will need lots of water-washed pebbles – as many as you can afford or gather.

DESIGN COMPONENTS

This design draws its inspiration from a 1950s-type seaside chalet community. The components are: a brightly painted wooden chalet (possibly with bunk beds), a porch and/or a small area of decking resembling a landing stage in front, a sand and pebble beach, a bit of scrubby grass, a shingle path and of course water.

IS IT RIGHT FOR YOUR GARDEN?

To get this design right, you need a good-sized, sloping garden in a sunny position, so that you can have the chalet hut on the high end, with a beach running down to the water. Is your garden big enough?

VARIATIONS TO CONSIDER

If you want to take the design further, you could build a large paddling pool with a beach, so that the whole garden becomes a seaside in miniature. You could style the whole set-up for children, so that they can paddle and splash, and generally have all the fun of the seaside.

MORE IDEAS

A rock pool can be exciting, especially for kids, and can be created in a weekend.

A 'seashore' fountain complete with driftwood, shells, seaweed and shingle.

Wooden boards can be fixed in a variety of patterns, and painted an appropriate colour.

Design guidelines for success

- You need the largest possible pond with a sand and pebble beach.

- You need a chalet that looks like something out of the 1950s, with items such as fishing and shrimping nets, glass floats and beachcombing finds draped around it.

- The chalet is best built on a slight rise, or raised up on short stilts.

- The area from the chalet down to the water must look like a beach, with lots of sand and shingle.

- Use bleached-wood fencing or canvas screens as a backdrop to the chalet.

- Plant a few trees, such as pines or palms, and scrubby grasses, as well as some coastal plants.

- A small area of decking in front of the chalet makes a good sitting area.

HOW TO CREATE A SEASIDE GARDEN

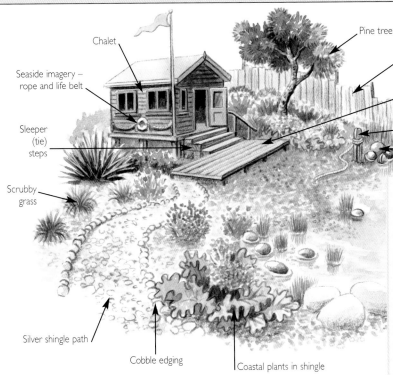

Chalet

Pine tree

Seaside imagery –
rope and life belt

Weatherboard fence

Landing-stage decking

Mooring post

Collection of floats

Sleeper
(tie)
steps

Scrubby
grass

Silver shingle path

Cobble edging

Coastal plants in shingle

CARE AND MAINTENANCE

The whole seaside effect depends upon the water being clear, so you will have to make sure that the pump and filter are always in good working condition.

Since the pond is free of fish and plants, you could throw a handful or two of salt into the water.

Remove leaves and debris, and make sure that muddy feet are kept back from the pool.

Bring frost-tender plants in for the winter.

Keep adding sand and shingle to the area around the chalet.

Give the chalet and fences a very thin wash of matt (latex) white paint so that they look sun-bleached and weather-worn.

For this project, you will need a site that is about 15 m (50 ft) wide and 30 m (100 ft) long, ideally sloping down to the water area.

Order of work

• Draw up your designs so that they take into account the house, the boundaries, immovable structures, drains and large trees.
• Give unwanted plants away or dispose of them.
• Fence the space with high wooden weatherboard panels.
• Build a large, shallow pond at the low end of the site. Use a flexible liner, with the edges of the liner hidden from view under shingle and sand.
• Sculpt the whole area with fine shingle, pea gravel and washed sand.
• Install a pump and filter to keep the water clear (see the pump and filter diagram on page 11, bottom right).
• Build the chalet on the rising ground so that it overlooks the pond; if the ground is flat, raise the chalet up on short legs.
• Plant small areas of scrubby grass around the chalet.
• Plant coastal plants such as *Cistus laurifolius* (Rock Rose), *Crambe maritima* (Sea Kale) and *Santolina chamaecyparissus* (Cotton Lavender) – anything that looks as if it belongs on a mild but windy beach. Plant frost-tender plants such as agaves in containers.

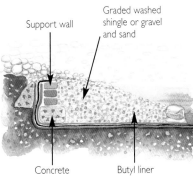

Support wall

Graded washed
shingle or gravel
and sand

Concrete

Butyl liner

↗ *Cross-section of a pond with a beach area on one side – the construction must be hidden.*

Development

You could theme in and around the chalet – wooden shingles on the roof, bits and pieces of driftwood. You could have beachcombed items like old rope, logs and bits of chain on the outside, and things like glass fishing floats, anchors and fishing nets on the inside. If you live near the sea, you could search out a damaged rowing boat, and have a bucket of seaweed. You could collect boot- or garage-sale items to furnish the chalet – lamp, anchor, shell pictures – anything that speaks of the sea. You could also have some bunk beds inside the chalet for the children to sleep in.

Cottage-style water garden

A cottage garden is a romantic mishmash of vegetable plots, chicken runs, apple trees and compost heaps, with lots of meandering paths and herbs and wild flowers all around. This water garden contains all these traditional elements, with the addition of water and a more organized arrangement for vegetables. You could have water troughs, a well, a large hand pump, a natural pond or whatever takes your fancy. There are many exciting options.

Is this traditional?

FRUIT, VEGETABLES AND WATER

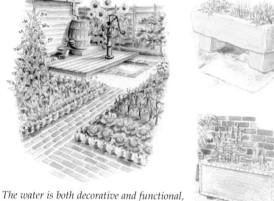

A genuine stone coffin makes a good trough for housing a raised water garden.

The water is both decorative and functional, which is good for a working garden.

Using an old galvanized water cistern set on a brick plinth is a quick way to make a water feature.

You could make a moving water garden using half-barrels and a pump.

DESIGN COMPONENTS

While the design needs to contain both water and a kitchen garden, the emphasis can be shifted to favour one or the other of these two elements. You will need to decide on the balance that is right for you.

IS IT RIGHT FOR YOUR GARDEN?

A garden of this character can be shaped to suit just about any site, but the vegetables will do best when the site is sunny and sheltered. The question to ask yourself is – do you like growing food enough to make the most of it?

VARIATIONS TO CONSIDER

You could have a large pond with just a small patch of vegetables, a massive kitchen-garden area with a small water feature, a courtyard full of vegetables and with a spouting mask (see pages 37 and 39), or lines of vegetables around a large pond – it all depends upon the size and character of your garden.

MORE IDEAS

Cut-away diagram showing how to build a false wishing well, which can make an excellent feature for a small garden.

Design guidelines for success

• There needs to be a clear decision on your part as to how big you want the kitchen-garden component to be.

• The vegetables need a sunny, sheltered site – not too many overhanging trees or blasting winds.

• A traditional walled garden is a good option, especially if you are starting out with a walled site.

• Small raised beds are good – they are easier to work and they contain the growing area much better than large, open beds.

• You can save on time and effort by improving the soil. A good method is to bring in mushroom compost and well-rotted manure, so that you can start out with a good growing mix.

• Plan out a pattern of paths so that you can use a wheelbarrow, and so that the beds are properly contained.

HOW TO CREATE A COTTAGE-STYLE WATER GARDEN

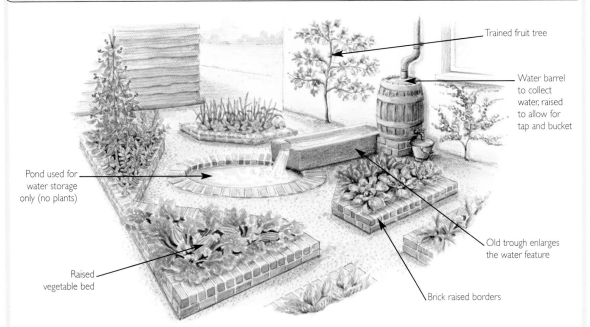

Trained fruit tree

Water barrel to collect water, raised to allow for tap and bucket

Pond used for water storage only (no plants)

Old trough enlarges the water feature

Raised vegetable bed

Brick raised borders

If growing vegetables is your primary interest, but you want the garden to be both functional and decorative, this design will be a good one for you.

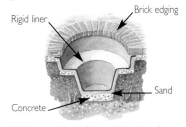

Rigid liner

Brick edging

Sand

Concrete

↗ *Cross-section of a rigid-liner pond (in this case the shelf will not be used).*

Order of work

• Draw up your designs so that they take into account the house, the boundaries, immovable structures, drains and large trees.
• Give unwanted plants away or dispose of them.
• Mark out the geometrical pattern of paths and borders.
• Put walls or fence panels around the whole site.
• Build the raised edges for the vegetable beds.
• Cover the paths with compacted hardcore, followed by gravel or crushed bark.

• Top up the vegetable beds with a mix of mushroom compost and well-rotted manure.
• Position the oak barrel to take water from the house (and optional trough), and then build the sunken pond to take the overflow from the barrel.
• Arrange any compost containers (not shown here).
• Build or erect the shed and/or greenhouse (not shown here).
• Plant fruit trees close to the boundaries so that you can train them to shape.
• Plant various crops in due season.

CARE AND MAINTENANCE

In a kitchen garden, care and maintenance are ongoing and managed according to season. The whole process is a continuous one of planting, weeding, harvesting, soil preparation, replanting and so on.

The paths and edgings need to be kept in good order.

The barrel, trough and sunken pond will need to be cleaned out at regular intervals – best in winter when they swiftly refill.

Let selected beds rest.

Remove leaves and debris and add them to the compost heap.

Make sure that the paths are kept clear so that you can use and enjoy the garden with maximum efficiency.

Development

You could really go to town with the water-saving and include several sunken ponds and barrels. You could arrange the water containers around the site so that they are conveniently to hand. You could collect old and decorative but useful gardening items, such as a mobile water-carrier – a sort of metal water butt on wheels.

Choosing water-garden plants

There are plants for every watery situation: waterside plants to complement and shelter the pond, bog plants for the damp ground around the water's edge, emergent or marginal plants for the shallows, floating-leaf and deep-water plants for a whole range of depths, and aquatic plants that either float or are completely or partially submerged. In this section, any plants that happen to fall into more than one category are cross-referenced.

USING PLANTS IN YOUR WATER GARDEN

Objective Plants are chosen not only for their inherent qualities but also for their dramatic effect – to give height, breadth and colour to the overall scene, to provide scent, to oxygenate the water, to provide food and cover for pondlife, and so on.

Water features Designing a flower bed can be seen as 'embellishing with plants', chosen according to their colour, size, character and habit; in just the same way, plants are chosen to embellish the water.

Scale Look at the labels and try to visualize how the mature plant will relate to the overall character of the pond. Will it be too big? Would it be better to go for a smaller variety?

Style To a great extent, style has to do with preconceived notions. For example, waterlilies might conjure up pictures of Monet paintings, whereas reeds speak of natural lakes.

Location Plants thrive when they are planted in conditions that suit their nature, so always read the labels before setting them in position. This is especially important in the context of water plants.

Design Be mindful that, in terms of design, plants are multi-dimensional – they not only have height, width and depth, they also have history, colour, form and scent.

Planned informality is the key to achieving a successful look with a wild natural water garden.

WATER-GARDEN PLANT GROUPS

In this book, plants are divided into the following five groups.

Floating-leaf plants
Plants that variously float on the surface; these give cover to spawning fish and aquatic insects.

Aquatic plants
Plants that give off bubbles of oxygen; these are good for keeping the water clear and using up waste nutrients.

Bog and moisture-loving plants
Plants that thrive in wet or waterlogged soil; these provide cover for frogs and insects.

Backdrop plants
Just about any plant – tree, bush, shrub or flower – that you consider complements the water garden.

Emergent or marginal plants
Plants that thrive at the water's edge or in shallow water; these provide cover for fish and frogs.

What to buy

First assess the size and character of your water garden, and then, armed with a pencil and pad, visit as many water gardens as you can find.

How many to buy

Plants not only grow in size, they can also be increased from seed or cuttings, or begged from friends. You could buy a few choice items and then get the rest when the time is right, or you could buy the lot in one go and give the thinnings away later.

Where to buy

Plants are best purchased from garden centres and nurseries that specialize in the various categories of water-garden plants.

COMBINING PLANTS

The five groups will furnish plants for each area within the water garden. Whereas a large pond will require specific choices from all five groups, so that an ecological balance can be achieved, a small water feature might well only need to be embellished with generalized plants.

General terms and what they mean

Annual plant Annuals are sown, grow and flower in the space of one year.

Biennial plant Biennials are sown one year and flower the next.

Container plant Any plant that will happily grow in a container.

Deciduous Foliage-bearing trees and shrubs that lose all their leaves at the end of the growing season.

Evergreen Foliage-bearing trees and shrubs that are in a state of continually shedding and replacing leaves.

Hardy Plants that are able to withstand cold, frosty conditions.

Herbaceous perennial Plants that die down to ground level in autumn and produce fresh shoots in spring. These plants usually live for 3–4 years before they need to be lifted and divided.

Rock and scree plants There is a huge range of plants that thrive in rock, scree and desert situations – everything from hardy alpines and dwarf trees through to cacti and succulents.

Shrub A woody, perennial plant smaller than a tree and with several stems growing from ground level.

Tree A large, woody, perennial plant giving rise to branches and leaves some distance from the ground.

PLANTING SCHEMES

Every type of water garden, because of its size, character, depth of water or quality of water, requires an individual planting scheme. For example, while a large, informal pond looks its best when it is furnished with a wide range of waterside and pond plants that are natural to the area, a small, seaside water garden needs to be furnished with plants that say more about the theme. The following are suggestions for different types of water garden.

Small, formal, shallow pond with a small fountain

For a depth of about 45 cm (18 in):

FLOATING-LEAF – *Stratiotes aloides* (Water Soldier)
AQUATIC – *Utricularia vulgaris* (Bladderwort), *Ceratophyllum* spp. (Hornwort)

Natural pond with fish

A natural pond needs a full range of plants:

BACKDROP – *Salix* spp. (Willows – varieties native to your area)
BOG – *Miscanthus sinensis* 'Zebrinus' (Striped Grass) and *Osmunda regalis* (Royal Fern)
EMERGENT – *Iris ensata* 'Ol' Man River' (Japanese Flag), *Glyceria maxima* (Sweet Grass)
FLOATING-LEAF – *Myriophyllum aquaticum* (Parrot's Feather), *Azolla caroliniana* (Fairy Moss)
AQUATIC – *Potamogeton crispus* (Curled Pondweed), *Fontinalis antipyretica* (Willow Moss)

Slow, meandering meadow stream

A slow stream can be planted with a full range of plants:

BACKDROP – *Salix alba* 'Britzensis' (Coral-bark Willow), *Acer* spp. (Maples), *Cornus* spp. (Dogwoods)
BOG AND MOISTURE-LOVING – *Osmunda regalis* (Royal Fern), *Iris* spp., *Hosta* spp.
EMERGENT – *Iris ensata* 'Ol' Man River' (Japanese Flag), *Glyceria maxima* (Sweet Grass), *Ranunculus lingua* (Greater Spearwort)
FLOATING-LEAF – *Myriophyllum aquaticum* (Parrot's Feather)

and *Marsilea* spp. (Water Clover)
AQUATIC – *Potamogeton crispus* (Curled Pondweed), *Nitella* spp. (Stonewort)

Fast-flowing mountain stream

No plants in the water, and all other plants must be kept well back from the water:

BACKDROP – *Salix babylonica* (Babylon Weeping Willow), *Betula* spp. (Birches), *Cornus alba* 'Sibirica' (Dogwood)
BOG AND MOISTURE-LOVING – *Asclepias incarnata* (Swamp Milkweed), *Astilbe* spp.

Japanese water garden

BACKDROP – *Salix babylonica* (Weeping Willow), *Acer palmatum* (Japanese Maple), *Bambusa multiplex* 'Riviereorum' (Bamboo), *Tsuga canadensis* (Canadian Hemlock)
BOG AND MOISTURE-LOVING – *Osmunda regalis* (Royal Fern), *Athyrium filix-femina* (Lady Fern), *Cyperus alternifolius* (Umbrella Plant; but note that this plant is not hardy outdoors in temperate climates), *Eriophorum* spp. (Cotton Grass)
EMERGENT – *Calla palustris* (Bog Arum), *Iris laevigata*
FLOATING-LEAF – *Azolla caroliniana* (Fairy Moss), *Nuphar japonica* (Japanese Pond Lily), *Salvinia auriculata* (Butterfly Fern)
AQUATIC – *Potamogeton crispus* (Curled Pondweed), *Ranunculus aquatilis* (Water Buttercup)

Bog and moisture-loving plants

What precisely is a bog garden?

A bog garden is the gardener's equivalent of the soggy, low-lying areas around the edge of natural ponds, lakes and streams. In natural situations, and depending upon the country and region, such areas are packed full of plants like irises, *Gunnera manicata* and lilies. While the soil needs to be wet, the underlying water must be free-moving rather than stagnant. If you like water-loving wildlife, shade, abundance and informality, you will enjoy a bog garden.

GUIDELINES

There are plants suitable for every boggy situation: high-bog areas that partially dry out in high summer, mid-bog areas that are always slightly moist, and low-bog areas that are more water than bog. Some plants are so adaptable that they thrive in places that are liable to extremes of both flood and drought. Be aware that some bog plants are described and sold as emergent or marginal plants.

TIPS

If you have doubts about the suitability of a certain plant in a certain situation, have a trial run with a single plant to see how it thrives, and then plant larger groups accordingly. When using sheet plastic liners to create a bog garden, make sure they are pierced to allow water to drain away. The water within the bog needs to be moving, rather than still and stagnant.

Although a bog garden tends to be difficult for humans underfoot – soft and spongy – it is perfect for wildlife.

Adiantum venustum
Maidenhair Fern UK/USA

Fern with delicate, fan-like leaves. Not all these ferns are hardy enough outdoors in a temperate climate; check with your supplier before buying.

Soil and situation: moist soil in a warm, humid dappled-shade situation; good for the outer fringes of a sheltered bog area.

Design notes: fine for a large, naturally wooded area that runs right down to the water. The bright pink new growth and the delicate character make this an excellent choice for a Japanese garden.

↕ 25 cm (10 in) ↔ 30 cm (12 in)

Astilbe x arendsii 'Amethyst'

Herbaceous perennial with coppery red-green leaves and fluffy spires of lilac-pink flowers.

Soil and situation: wet soil (not waterlogged) in sun or dappled shade.

Design notes: the large size and wide range of dramatic colours make this a fine choice for a large, naturally wooded area that runs right down to the water.

↕ 90 cm (3 ft) ↔ 60 cm (2 ft)

Astrantia major 'Ruby Wedding'

Masterwort UK/USA

Herbaceous perennials with divided green leaves and lots of crimson, daisy-like flowers.

Soil and situation: moist soil that is not waterlogged, in sun or partial shade.

Design notes: good for a wooded, natural pond, when you want the trees to come right down to the water.

↕ 60 cm (2 ft) ↔ 45 cm (18 in)

Camassia cusickii

Quamash UK/USA

Summer-flowering bulb with long, bright green leaves and brilliant violet flowers.

Soil and situation: moist soil in sun or shade.

Design notes: excellent when you want a strong splash of colour; looks particularly good in large swathes.

 90 cm (3 ft) ↔ 30 cm (1 ft)

Canna 'Panache'

Spreading, frost-tender herbaceous perennial with purple-green leaves and brilliant pink-red flowers.

Soil and situation: likes a moist to wet soil. In a cold and frosty climate, the rhizomes need to be stored inside for the winter.

Design notes: a good option for a formal setting, such as in a damp bed around a formal pond, or in a bog garden that is fed from a pond. A very showy plant.

 1.2 m (4 ft) ↔ indefinite

Carex elata 'Aurea'

Bowles' Golden Sedge UK/USA

Sedge USA

Hardy, evergreen perennial with tufted, grassy foliage that produces small, brown-green flowers.

Soil and situation: deep, wet soil or shallow water in sun or shade.

Design notes: suitable for bog areas that run into the water. A good choice for a green theme, a Japanese garden, a meadow stream and a natural pond. It is sometimes sold as an emergent.

90 cm (3 ft) ↔ 90 cm (3 ft)

Cimicifuga simplex 'Frau Herms'

Bugbane UK/USA

Perennial with small, glossy leaves and small, delicate, white flowers on a long, wiry, rod-like stem.

Soil and situation: moist, shady site.

Design notes: a good choice for a large, natural woodland pond or a Japanese water garden.

 1.2 m (4 ft) ↔ 50 cm (20 in)

Crinum 'Cape Dawn'

Spreading plant with spiky, green leaves and exotic, pink-white flowers.

Soil and situation: likes a moist soil in dappled sun or full shade.

Design notes: the perfect choice for a Japanese water garden; it would look stunning alongside *Zantedeschia aethiopica* (Arum Lily) and ferns.

60 cm (2 ft) ↔ indefinite

Eriophorum angustifolium

Cotton Grass UK/USA

Green-tufted, evergreen grass with little, fluffy, cotton-ball flowers.

Soil and situation: deep, moist, acid soil or water to a depth of 5 cm (2 in).

Design notes: good for areas that run from wet bog to shallow water; the delicate appearance makes it suitable for a Japanese or Chinese garden.

60 cm (2 ft) ↔ indefinite

Houttuynia cordata '**Chameleon**'

Spreading herbaceous perennial with red stems and sweet-smelling, strikingly variegated leaves.

Soil and situation: wet soil or water to a depth of 5 cm (2 in) in sun or dappled shade.

Design notes: a good choice for ground cover for a large, natural, lightly wooded area that runs right down to the water. It can be invasive, so you either need lots of space or you have to keep cutting it back.

↕ 60 cm (2 ft) ↔ indefinite

Juncus effusus '**Spiralis**'
Corkscrew Rush UK/USA

Contorted, dark green perennial with lots of semi-prostrate, dark green, twisting and curling stems. It has green-brown flower tufts in summer.

Soil and situation: wet boggy ground or shallow water.

Design notes: this plant is excellent for bog gardens that run into the water and/or areas that are subject to flooding.

↕ 90 cm (3 ft) ↔ 60 cm (2 ft)

Lysichiton americanus
Yellow Skunk Cabbage UK/USA

Western Skunk Cabbage USA

Vigorous, deciduous herbaceous perennial with spectacular, large, brilliant yellow, blade-shaped spathes.

Soil and situation: very moist soil or water to a depth of 2.5 cm (1 in) in sun or shade.

Design notes: a good option for a large, naturally wooded area that runs right down to the water, or for a small, exhibition bog area when you are trying to create a dramatic wooded look.

↕ 1.2 m (4 ft) ↔ 90 cm (3 ft)

Orontium aquaticum
Golden Club UK/USA

Herbaceous perennial with blue-green leaves and poker-like, yellow-orange flowers. The leaves are quite unusual in that they have a silver-grey sheen on the underside.

Soil and situation: deep, wet soil or water to a depth of about 30 cm (1 ft) in sun or shade.

Design notes: good for a large, lush bog area that runs into the water – it is sometimes sold as an emergent. If you plant it on the water-line, it will grow both in and out of the water.

↕ 45 cm (18 in) ↔ 60 cm (2 ft)

Pennisetum orientale
Chinese Fountain Grass UK/USA

Herbaceous perennial with slender, grassy, green leaves and fluffy, delicate, purple-white flowers.

Soil and situation: moist to well-drained soil in a sunny position.

Design notes: a good choice when you want to concentrate on growing grasses and green papyrus-like plants. Ideal for a Mediterranean-type water garden where the soil is moist.

↕ 90 cm (3 ft) ↔ 25 cm (10 in)

Phragmites australis
Common Reed USA

Carrizo USA

Reed-like grass with long green leaves that also produces small, purple flowers.

Soil and situation: deep, wet soil or water to a depth of about 50 cm (2 in) in sun or shade.

Design notes: this plant is a good choice for bog areas that run into the water, and is really good for a large, natural pond and/or when you want to achieve a cool green theme. It is sometimes described and sold as an emergent (see page 53).

↕ 45 cm (18 in) ↔ 60 cm (2 ft)

Ranunculus macrophyllus
Greater Spearwort UK

Delicate but tall herbaceous perennial with clusters of buttercup flowers.

Soil and situation: likes wet soil in sun or shade. The soil needs to be moist, but not so wet that there is standing water.

Design notes: looks its best in a wooded situation, on the fringes of a natural pond.

↥ 1.8 m (6 ft) ↔ 1.5 m (5 ft)

Rodgersia pinnata 'Superba'

Hardy herbaceous perennial with bronze-green leaves and tall plumes of deep pink-red flowers.

Soil and situation: deep, rich, moist soil in sun or shade.

Design notes: a good choice for a large, naturally wooded area that runs right down to the water, when there is a lot of space. It is also useful when you want to create a dramatic, showy effect, for a Chinese garden, or as a small detail in the corner of a Japanese garden.

↥ 90 cm (3 ft) ↔ 90 cm (3 ft)

Schizostylis coccinea 'Major'
Crimson Flag USA

Spreading herbaceous perennial with green, grassy foliage and masses of bright crimson flowers; it has been described as looking like a small gladiolus.

Soil and situation: does best in deep, rich, wet soil or in water to a depth of 10 cm (4 in) in sun or shade. It must be sheltered from wind.

Design notes: a good option for a large area that runs right down to the water. The long flowering season (mid-autumn to late winter) makes it a fine choice for a large, sheltered garden.

↥ 60 cm (2 ft) ↔ indefinite

Solidago 'Golden Shower'
Golden Rod UK/USA

Herbaceous perennial with feathery, green leaves and large, yellow, spire-like flowers at the end of a long stem.

Soil and situation: well-draining, moist soil in sun or shade.

Design notes: an excellent choice when you want to create a big effect in a short time. The golden-yellow flowers are big and bold – perfect when you are trying to cover newly dug ground.

↥ 1.5 m (5 ft) ↔ 90 cm (3 ft)

Trollius x cultorum 'Orange Princess'

Herbaceous perennial with deeply cleft, dark green leaves and fat, ball-shaped, orange-yellow, buttercup-like flowers.

Soil and situation: moist soil in sun or dappled shade.

Design notes: a good choice for a large, natural-looking area that runs right down to a pond, or strung out in clumps alongside a meandering stream.

↥ 90 cm (3 ft) ↔ 60 cm (2 ft)

Viola cucullata
Marsh Blue Violet USA

Wood Violet UK/USA

Spreading perennial with purple-green leaves that bears lavender-purple flowers in spring and summer.

Soil and situation: moist but well-drained soil in sun or shade. The soil should be moist rather than saturated.

Design notes: a good choice for a large, naturally wooded area that runs right down to the water. The very delicate flowers would look good alongside a small, raised pond.

↥ 15 cm (6 in) ↔ indefinite

Emergent (marginal) plants

What does 'emergent' mean?

Emergent plants, also known as marginals, grow along the water's edge. They are plants that grow in the shallows of slow-flowing water such as streams, ponds and canals. Depending upon the specific type, emergent plants flourish in very moist soil through to water that ranges in depth from 5 to 75 cm (2–30 in). Characteristically, they can withstand short alternating periods of drought and flood. Well-planted emergents blur the line between land and water.

GUIDELINES

For some emergent plants, the depth of water is critical. If you have any doubts about the correct water depth, start by planting in the shallows and see how each plant thrives. Emergents are perfect for 'natural' ponds, especially when you are trying to encourage wildlife to colonize the area. They give cover for small creatures, as well as providing an excellent breeding ground for a variety of insects.

TIPS

Some emergents are vigorous, to the extent that at some point you will have to thin them out and/or contain their roots within wire baskets. If the pond has a thin plastic liner, you should be very wary about plants that have sharp, spiky roots, such as *Typha* spp. (Reedmace).

There are irises to suit every growing situation – from slightly moist soil through to deep water, and from full sunshine to shade.

Acorus calamus 'Variegatus'
Myrtle Flag UK/USA

Sweet Flag UK/USA

Herbaceous perennial with green-cream, iris-like leaves; it produces minute flowers on the end of the leaf tips. The leaves are slightly scented when rubbed.

Soil and situation: likes having its roots in water, up to a depth of 23 cm (9 in), in sun or shade.

Design notes: a good option for a large, natural pond, or a formal pond when you want a green theme; it looks good set against pebbles and brick.

↕ 75 cm (30 in) ↔ 60 cm (2 ft)

Cyperus involucratus
Paper Reed Papyrus UK/USA

Evergreen perennial with a delicate collection of spray-like heads; flowers appear on the ends of the sprays.

Soil and situation: likes having its roots in water, up to a depth of 25 cm (10 in), in sun or shade; does not like a windy site.

Design notes: good for a large, natural pond, or a formal pond. It would look at home in a Mediterranean-type garden, or when you are looking for grassy, palm-like plants.

↕ 38 cm (15 in) ↔ 90 cm (3 ft)

Iris ensata 'Ol' Man River'
Japanese Flag UK

Sword Iris USA

Vigorous, spreading, herbaceous, clump-forming perennial with broad, blue-green leaves and brilliant violet-blue flowers.

Soil and situation: in summer likes having its roots in water, up to a depth of 7.5 cm (3 in), in sun or shade.

Design notes: a wonderful choice for a large, natural pond. Looks perfect in a densely wooded setting. Irises are a good option if you want to specialize in a single plant or colour theme – there are lots of sizes and colours.

↕ 60 cm (2 ft) ↔ indefinite

Iris pseudacorus

Yellow Flag Iris UK/USA

Spreading herbaceous perennial with upright, sword-like leaves and beautiful, characteristic, yellow flowers.

Soil and situation: sometimes sold as a bog plant as it can do well in very wet soil, it does best when its roots are in water, up to a depth of 30 cm (1 ft), in sun or shade. Likes a deep, rich soil.

Design notes: a wonderful option when you want a vigorous plant to run right through a bog garden and on into the water. Good for a large, natural pond or slow, meandering stream.

↕ 1.2 m (4 ft) ↔ indefinite

Iris sibirica

Siberian Iris UK/USA

Herbaceous perennial with narrow, grass-like leaves and exotic, dark-veined, violet-blue flowers.

Soil and situation: adaptable – likes having its roots on dry ground or in water, up to a depth of 5 cm (2 in), in sun or shade.

Design notes: a good choice for a large, natural pond or stream, or a wet bog garden that has a history of drying out. Good if you want to collect irises.

↕ 45 cm (18 in) ↔ 90 cm (3 ft)

Lobelia cardinalis

Herbaceous perennial with green foliage and brilliant red flowers on a tall, spire-like stem.

Soil and situation: although this is sometimes described and sold as a bog plant, because it can do well in very wet soil, it does best when its roots are in water, up to a depth of 10 cm (4 in), in sun or shade. Likes a deep, rich soil.

Design notes: good if you want a dramatic swathe of colour to run right through a bog garden and on into the water. The colour is stunning. Flowers last from mid- to very late summer.

↕ 90 cm (3 ft) ↔ 30 cm (1 ft)

Phragmites australis 'Variegatus'

Swamp-loving, spreading perennial with long, green-yellow leaves and stems, and glossy, purple flower plumes in summer.

Soil and situation: sometimes sold as a bog plant (see page 50), but it does best when its roots are in water up to a depth of 1.5 m (5 ft), in sun or shade. Likes a deep, rich soil.

Design notes: ideal for a wild pond, a Japanese garden, or when you want a green theme. Looks good in clumps, or as swathes running from the bog garden into deep water. Needs lots of space.

↕ 4 m (13 ft) ↔ indefinite

Zantedeschia aethiopica

Arum Lily UK/USA

Common Calla USA

Pig Lily USA

Half-hardy plant with deep green, glossy leaves and the most beautiful, cream-white, trumpet-shaped flowers.

Soil and situation: happy in a wet bog garden, or as an emergent with its roots in water, up to a depth of 15 cm (6 in) in sun or shade.

Design notes: a good choice for a large, natural pond, for a formal pond, or if you want to create a bold impression. Would look good in a Japanese garden.

↕ 1 m (3½ ft) ↔ 45 cm (18 in)

OTHER EMERGENT PLANTS

- *Alisma plantago-aquatica* (**Water Plantain**): herbaceous perennial with pink-white flowers on long stalks that does well in deep shallows – good food for wildlife.
- *Lysichiton americanus* (**Yellow Skunk Cabbage**): vigorous herbaceous perennial that does well grown as a bog plant (see page 50) or in still or moving shallow water.
- *Menyanthes trifoliata* (**Bog Bean, Marsh Trefoil**): herbaceous perennial with dark olive-green leaves and small, daisy-like flowers that is happy in shallow water; a good choice for a wild pond.
- *Pontederia cordata* (**Pickerel Weed**): vigorous, herbaceous perennial with heart-shaped leaves and delicate, blue flowers. Looks well in clumps on the water's edge. Good for a wild pond.
- *Saururus cernuus* (**Swamp Lily, Water Dragon**): herbaceous perennial with heart-shaped, green leaves and waxy, cream flowers on a spiky stem; it thrives in the deeper shallows.

Floating-leaf plants

These attractive plants have leaves and flowers that float on the surface of the water, and roots that either trail or anchor into the mud at the bottom of the pond. They are winners on two counts: they provide cover for wildlife, and they hold back the growth of algae. Of all the floating-leaf plants, waterlilies are arguably the most popular and colourful. If you want to encourage pondlife to colonize your water garden, you will need to include some floating-leaf plants.

What are floating-leaf plants?

GUIDELINES

Most floating-leaf plants are sensitive when it comes to water depth and water temperature. Make sure you read the labels. You need to know the depth and average water temperature of your pond. There are lots of waterlilies to choose from: pick ones that flower at different times. Unless otherwise stated here, the plants remain at the level of the water's surface.

TIPS

Be careful not to damage your pond when you are positioning the plants; do not use spikes, garden forks or sticks. Some of these plants are very choosy when it comes to the character of the water – cold, warm, moving, still and so on – so read the labels. If you have doubts about the suitability of a particular plant, buy a small one and see how it does.

With its heavy-scented, semi-double flowers with deep pink petals and golden stamens, this waterlily is perfect for a large pond.

Azolla caroliniana

Fairy Moss UK/USA

Water Fern UK/USA

Minute, free-floating, spreading perennial that forms clustering colonies of tiny green to purple-brown leaves.

Situation: likes to float freely on the water.

Design notes: a good plant for a new pond. You can use it for swift cover while more slow-growing plants are becoming established. Can become invasive and crowd out everything else in the pond.

 indefinite

Nymphaea 'A. Siebert"

Waterlily UK/USA

Free-flowering tropical waterlily with brown to green-purple leaves and blue-purple flowers with yellow stamens. This plant needs a warm climate.

Situation: likes shallow water, to a depth of 60 cm (2 ft).

Design notes: a delicate lily with an unusual shimmer to the colour.

↔ 2.1 m (7 ft)

Nymphaea 'Attraction'

Waterlily UK/USA

Free-flowering waterlily with spotted, green-purple leaves and star-shaped, orange-red flowers with yellow stamens. (It can be difficult to obtain.)

Situation: likes plenty of space, in water to a depth of 90 cm (36 in).

Design notes: the delicate flowers nicely contrast with the splotchy leaves.

↔ 1.5 m (5 ft)

Nymphaea 'Ellisiana'

Waterlily UK/USA

Popular waterlily with green-purple leaves and rose-red-purple flowers with yellow stamens.

Situation: likes shallow water, to a depth of 45 cm (18 in).

Design notes: a good choice for small ponds and containers, but it also looks great when planted in rampant swathes.

 1.2 m (4 ft)

Nymphaea 'René Gérard'

Waterlily UK/USA

Large waterlily with large, brown to green-purple leaves and pink-flecked, rose-red flowers.

Situation: likes medium-deep water, to a depth of 45 cm (18 in), and plenty of space.

Design notes: a good choice for a large pond.

 1.5 m (5 ft)

Nymphoides peltata

Fringed Waterlily UK

Deciduous waterlily with small, green leaves and fringed, yellow flowers.

Situation: likes shallow water, to a depth of 45 cm (18 in).

Design notes: a good choice for a small, natural pond; it looks more homely than a large lily.

60 cm (2 ft)

Pistia stratiotes

Water Lettuce UK/USA

Shellflower USA

Free-floating, spreading plant with spongy, green leaves that cluster in a rosette shape that looks a bit like a lettuce. Not hardy in a cold climate.

Situation: likes to float freely on the water, to a depth of 90 cm (3 ft).

Design notes: although this plant will provide swift cover, it can become invasive and crowd out everything else in the pond. A good option for a natural pond, or a small formal pond.

 30 cm (1 ft) ⟷ indefinite

Salvinia auriculata

Butterfly Fern UK

Perennial, spreading, free-floating tropical plant with fold upon fold of slightly hairy, pale green leaves that look a bit like clusters of green butterflies. Not hardy in a cold climate.

Situation: floating freely on the water.

Design notes: this plant can become invasive. The leaves break off to become new plants. Remove the leaves as they brown off and die. A good option for a natural pond, or a small, formal pond; a bad idea for a stream.

↑ 25 cm (1 in) ⟷ indefinite

OTHER WATERLILIES

- *Nymphaea* **'Froebelii':** classic waterlily with brown to bronze-red green leaves and red-purple flowers with red-orange stamens. Water depth: 15–45 cm (6–18 in).
- *Nymphaea* **'Gladstoneana':** free-flowering waterlily with brown to green-purple leaves and cream-white flowers with yellow stamens. Water depth: 45–90 cm (18–36 in).
- *Nymphaea* **'Laydekeri Fulgens':** free-flowering waterlily with brown to green-purple, splotched leaves and deep red-purple flowers with red-orange stamens. Water depth: 15–45 cm (6–18 in).
- *Nymphaea* **'Lucida':** free-flowering waterlily with brown to green-purple, oval leaves and red-pink flowers with yellow stamens. Water depth: 45–60 cm (18–24 in).
- *Nymphaea* **'Virginalis':** free-flowering waterlily with green-purple leaves and cream-yellow flowers with yellow stamens. A delicate lily with unusual, narrow petals. Water depth: 15–45 cm (6–18 in).

Aquatic plants

Although there is some crossover between aquatics and floating-leaf plants, the difference is that aquatics have rooting systems that dissolve and absorb nutrients. Some aquatics float, while others are partially or totally submerged. Aquatics clean up the water in two ways: firstly they feed on all the rubbish at the bottom of the pond, and secondly they give off oxygen. If you want to have clear, high-quality water in your pond, you will need some aquatics.

GUIDELINES

You have two choices if you want clear water – you can install a pump and filter, or you can plant underwater aquatics. It is best to try just a few plants of different types and sizes, and see whether they thrive. If the water in your new pond is cloudy with mud or likely to be polluted with cement powder, hold back on the planting until the pond has settled down.

TIPS

Some of these plants are very specific when it comes to the character of the water. For example, some need warm, shallow, still water, while others like deep mud and shade. Read the labels carefully. Be careful when you are bringing in new plants that they are healthy and free from pests. It is a good idea to rinse them in clean water before you put them in the pond.

Eichhornia *(Water Hyacinth) floats on the surface and produces orchid-like blooms in late summer. It needs protection in winter.*

Ceratophyllum demersum
Spreading perennial with slender, brush-like fronds and small, pinkish flowers.

Situation: likes a shady pond, to a depth of 60 cm (24 in).

Design notes: a good plant for a formal or natural pond.

↔ indefinite

Fontinalis antipyretica
Water Moss USA
Willow Moss UK

Pretty, moss-like, spreading perennial, with long, hairy, dark green stems and little, spear-shaped leaves.

Situation: likes moving water, to a depth of 60 cm (24 in).

Design notes: a good choice for a running stream or spring.

↔ indefinite

Hottonia palustris
Feather Foil USA
Feather Violet USA
Water Violet UK

Pretty, spreading perennial, with masses of soft pale green leaves and pale pink-white flowers.

Situation: likes plenty of space, to a depth of 45 cm (18 in).

Design notes: an attractive plant; the flowers stand up above the surface of the water in spring.

↕ 90 cm (3 ft) ↔ indefinite

Myriophyllum aquaticum

Parrot Feather UK/USA

Water Feather USA

Spreading plant with feathery, green leaves on stems.

Situation: likes lots of space, to a depth of 60 cm (2 ft).

Design notes: good for a medium-depth natural pond. Grows fast, to the extent that it will push out of the water to mass against the sides of the pond.

 indefinite

Potamogeton crispus

Curled Pondweed UK

Pondweed USA

Spreading perennial with frond-like leaves and little, red and white flowers that just break the surface of the water.

Situation: likes to root in deep mud in still, shady water, to a depth of 90 cm (3 ft).

Design notes: a good plant for a large natural pond, where the roots can grow in the mud – where there are trees overhanging the water.

 indefinite

Ranunculus aquatilis

Crowfoot USA

Water Buttercup UK

Pretty, spreading, delicate annual or perennial, with small, green leaves and white-yellow flowers.

Situation: likes to root in deep mud, to a depth of 82 cm (32 in).

Design notes: good for a natural pond, where the roots can grow in the mud.

indefinite

Utricularia vulgaris

Bladderwort UK/USA

Hardy, spreading perennial, with brownish-green leaves, insect-catching bladders and yellow flowers.

Situation: likes deep water, to a depth of 1.2 m (4 ft).

Design notes: a good plant for a natural wildlife pond, that is unusual, exotic and eye-catching.

 indefinite

Vallisneria spiralis

Eelgrass UK/USA

Tape Grass UK/USA

Delicate, spreading perennial with long, strap- or tape-like leaves that have a twist or spiral along their length.

Situation: likes shallow still water, to a depth of 30 cm (1 ft).

Design notes: a good choice for a pond where you want plants just breaking the surface of the water.

indefinite

OTHER AQUATIC PLANTS

- *Bacopa* spp. (Water Hyssop): submerged aquatics with green-pink leaves and bright blue flowers – good for a small, sunny pond.
- *Hippuris vulgaris* (Mare's Tail, Bottle Brush, Knotgrass): plant with whorls of green leaves on vertical stems, like little brushes; it is good for a large, natural pond as it needs lots of space.
- *Lagarosiphon major*: semi-evergreen with masses of snake-like stems covered in tiny scale-like leaves; good for large areas of deep water.
- *Lemna* spp. (Duckweed): plants with minute leaves that form a green carpet upon the surface of the water; they make good food for wildlife in a large, natural pond.
- *Myriophyllum verticillatum* (Milfoil): perennial with fat stems with rings of bright green leaves; good for large areas of shallow water.
- *Nitella* (syn. *Chara*) spp. (Stonewort): primitive plants, related to algae, with greyish-green, spiky foliage, that are good for clearing the water.

Backdrop plants

Every water garden needs a backdrop of trees, shrubs and other plants to provide shade, privacy and shelter for all the wildlife that will inevitably come to the water. Moreover, the height, colour and general character of certain plants can say more about a water garden than a thousand words. Willows speak of English streams and village ponds, while delicate maples and fluffy grasses are perfect for a Japanese water garden. These plants link the water to the garden.

GUIDELINES

The first thing to do when planning out the planting is to list what your garden has to offer in the way of sun, shade, soil, water and shelter. Next, group the plants according to their various needs. This done, you will be able, by a process of elimination, to tell instantly which plants are going to be likely candidates. You will then be able to go to the nursery or garden centre armed with a shortlist. It is always a good idea to visit local water gardens for ideas and inspiration.

TIPS

The best tip when choosing plants is to wander around your neighbourhood and to take note of plants that do well. When you are visiting the garden centre or nursery, read the labels and take note of eventual size. You might like a willow, but is it going to outgrow your garden? You might want to plant a particular tree so that it is the first thing you see in the morning, but will it eventually cast too much shade? It is always advisable to try to think quite a long way ahead.

COMPLETING THE PICTURE

Focus on plants that attract your attention and then search out their names and needs.

The conifer Metasequoia glyptostroboides prefers to grow near streams and ponds.

Visit large gardens in your local area, or farther afield if you have the inclination and the time, and look for ideas – take notes, ask questions, and generally enjoy the experience.

Many kinds of bamboo are suitable for growing by water.

Ferns will grow on the margins of streams and ponds.

Miscanthus sinensis 'Zebrinus' (Zebra Grass) grows well in deeply dug, moist soil in bog gardens or alongside the water.

SETTING THE OVERALL SCENE

Salix babylonica *(Weeping Willow) trees are grown more for their shape than for anything else. They thrive in moist ground and look stunning beside a stretch of water.*

The hardy, moisture-loving Gunnera manicata *has enormous, dramatic leaves.*

x Hibanobambusa tranquillans 'Shiroshima' is a moisture-loving bamboo.

Bog gardens give the illusion of water, even if there are no actual ponds or streams present. Some of the better 'water gardens' are all bog and no water, relying on clever planting.

Blechnum chilense
Hard Fern UK

Delicate, primitive, moisture-loving fern with characteristic fronds.

Soil and situation: deep, rich, moist, lime-free soil in sun or dappled shade.

Design notes: a good choice for a wild garden, a 'primitive'-themed garden or for a green plant collection.

↕ 15–75 cm (6–30 in) ↔ 45–75 cm (18–30 in)

Campanula latifolia 'Brantwood'
Bellflower UK/USA

Perennial with deep green leaves and blue, grey or purple, bell-shaped flowers.

Soil and situation: deep, rich, moist, well-drained soil in sun or dappled shade.

Design notes: a good choice for bog gardens and woodland. There are so many types that it is possible to have bellflowers growing almost anywhere – at the water's edge, in woodland and even in areas of dry garden that are away from the water.

↕ 20 cm–1.2 m (8 in–4 ft) ↔ 90 cm (3 ft)

Chusquea culeou
Huge bamboo that has distinctive, jointed stems.

Soil and situation: deep, rich, moist soil in sun or partial shade.

Design notes: a fine plant for a large natural pond; it looks particularly good as a huge specimen plant.

↕ 6 m (20 ft) ↔ 2.4 m (8 ft)

Cimicifuga simplex
Bugbane UK/USA

Rattletop USA

Herbaceous perennial with wiry stems topped with fluffy, pink flowers.

Soil and situation: deep, rich, moist soil in a sunny situation, but will also grow in sheltered, dappled shade.

Design notes: a good choice for the water's edge, or for areas of deep shade under trees and shrubs.

↕ 1.2 m (4 ft) ↔ 50 cm (20 in)

Cornus alba 'Sibirica'
Dogwood UK

Siberian Dogwood USA

Deciduous shrub with green to yellow-red stems.

Soil and situation: deep, rich, moist soil in sun or shade.

Design notes: a good choice for a large, natural pond; it is grown for the colour of the stems.

↕ 1.8 m (6 ft) ↔ 3.5 m (12 ft)

Cortaderia selloana
Pampas Grass UK/USA

Huge, tussock-forming, evergreen perennial with beautiful, feathery, cream-white plumes. There are several good cultivars that vary in height and spread from the species.

Soil and situation: deep, rich, well-drained soil in a sunny situation.

Design notes: although a single plant would be a good choice, it looks its best in groups of 3–4. It needs plenty of space. Good as a backdrop to a large, natural pond or as a specimen plant in a small, walled garden.

↕ 3 m (10 ft) ↔ 3 m (10 ft)

Cyperus papyrus
Egyptian Reed Grass UK/USA

Papyrus UK/USA

Delicate, tall, tender grass with green-fringed, mop-like flowerheads.

Soil and situation: deep, rich, moist soil or water to a depth of 15 cm (6 in) in sun or dappled shade. Needs a warm, sheltered, frost-free position.

Design notes: looks its best alongside a natural pond, in a Mediterranean or Japanese garden, or as part of a collection of grasses. A good choice for a North African water garden.

↕ 4.8 m (16 ft) ↔ 90 cm (3 ft)

Dicksonia antarctica
Tasmanian Tree Fern USA

Tree Fern UK

Large, tree-like, tender fern with a trunk terminating in a huge rosette of divided fronds.

Soil and situation: deep, rich, warm, moist soil in a sunny, sheltered situation.

Design notes: a good choice for a large, natural pond in a sheltered position, or a sunny courtyard. Would look good as part of a tropical theme.

↕ 12 m (40 ft) ↔ 7.5 m (25 ft)

Equisetum spp.
Horsetails UK/USA

Scouring Rush USA

Delicate, primitive, rush-like perennials with jointed stems.

Soil and situation: deep, rich, moist, soil in a sunny situation.

Design notes: a good traditional choice for a large, wild, natural water garden. It looks stunning when allowed to run riot.

↕ 1.5 m (5 ft) ↔ 1.5 m (5 ft)

Eupatorium purpureum
Joe-pie Weed USA

Sweet Joe-pie Weed USA

Herbaceous perennial with green-purple stems topped with pink flowerheads.

Soil and situation: moist soil in sun or partial shade.

Design notes: a good choice for a sheltered garden; it grows into a good-sized plant.

↕ 2 m (6 ft) ↔ 90 cm (3 ft)

Hakonechloa macra
Delicate, mound-forming grass with red-tinted, gold-green leaves.

Soil and situation: deep, rich, moist soil in a sunny situation.

Design notes: good choice for a small pond in a sheltered, sunny garden, a small water garden, a Mediterranean or Japanese garden, or as part of a collection of grasses.

↕ 25 cm (10 in) ↔ 45 cm (18 in)

Hypericum spp.
St John's Wort UK/USA

Delicate ground-cover plants with soft, downy leaves and clusters of yellow flowers.

Soil and situation: deep, rich, well-drained soil in a sunny situation.

Design notes: a good traditional choice for a rock garden and as a ground-cover plant in a woodland.

↕ 30 cm (1 ft) ↔ indefinite

Iris spp.

Uniquely beautiful, spreading plants with long, green leaves and distinctive flowers. There are many to choose from, but not all are suitable for very wet soil – check with your supplier.

Soil and situation: deep, rich, moist soil or water to a depth of 15 cm (6 in) in sun or shade.

Design notes: the perfect plant for a water garden. There are so many types, sizes and colours that you could have a show of irises from spring through to late summer. A perfect mix would be irises, willows, ferns and grasses.

↕ 1.2 m (4 ft)   ↔ indefinite

Leucojum aestivum

Giant Snowflake USA

Summer Snowflake UK/USA

Pretty little bulbous perennial with slender, green leaves and bell-shaped, white flowers, much like a tall snowdrop.

Soil and situation: deep, rich, moist soil in sun or shade.

Design notes: the ideal plant for a wet area, when you are trying to achieve a natural wild look. Excellent option for a woodland water garden.

↕ 50 cm (20 in)   ↔ 30 cm (1 ft)

Osmunda regalis

Royal Fern UK

Royal Flowering Fern USA

Delicate, majestic fern with tall, green-russet fronds. Easy to grow.

Soil and situation: deep, rich, moist to boggy soil in sun or shade.

Design notes: looks fine close to the water, alongside irises, grasses and lilies. Also looks at home under tree cover.

↕ 1.8 m (6 ft)   ↔ 90 cm (3 ft)

Pennisetum spp.

Fountain Grass UK/USA

Delicate, perennial, clump- or mound-forming grasses with green leaves topped with feathery, purple plumes.

Soil and situation: rich, well-drained soil in a sunny situation set well back from the water where the soil is moist but not wet.

Design notes: a good traditional choice for an area of dry garden around a pond, or as feature plants within a walled garden. Looks fine alongside other grasses, and with ferns.

↕ 90 cm (3 ft)   ↔ 90 cm (3 ft)

Persicaria microcephala 'Red Dragon'

Bistort UK

Beautiful, spreading ground-cover plant with pointed, red-green leaves and small, pink-white flowers.

Soil and situation: moist soil.

Design notes: good for linking the bog garden to the pond, when you want to blur where the water starts and finishes.

↕ 10 cm (4 in)   ↔ indefinite

Phyllostachys spp.

Bamboos UK/USA

Large, spreading bamboos with grooved, branching stems and green-yellow leaves. There are many to choose from, with lots of different colours, heights and habits. Some can be invasive.

Soil and situation: deep, rich, moist soil in a sheltered, sunny or shady site.

Design notes: a good choice for a large to huge garden.

↕ 7.5 m (25 ft)   ↔ indefinite

Pleioblastus spp.

Bamboos UK/USA

Medium to small bamboos with jointed stems and green-yellow leaves.

Soil and situation: deep, rich, moist soil in a sheltered situation.

Design notes: a first-class choice when you want a compact, low-growing bamboo – good for a Chinese or Japanese water garden.

 90 cm (3 ft) ↔ indefinite

Polypodium vulgare

Common Fern UK

European Polypodium USA

Wall Fern USA

Delicate, attractive fern with green, leafy, spear-shaped stems.

Soil and situation: will grow just about anywhere, but prefers a deep, rich, moist soil in dappled shade.

Design notes: a good traditional choice for a green-themed garden, an enclosed water garden or a hothouse water garden.

↕ 45 cm (18 in) ↔ 45 cm (18 in)

Salix spp.

Willows UK/USA

Deciduous, water-loving trees with silvery, green-grey foliage and fluffy catkin flowers. There are lots of types and forms, from tall through to small and dwarf. Willows and water are made for each other.

Soil and situation: rich, moist soil in sun to dappled shade.

Design notes: a good traditional choice for a water garden. You will be able to get a variety to suit your space.

↕ 90 cm–25 m (3–80 ft) ↔ 1.5–12 m (5–40 ft)

Taxodium distichum

Pond Cypress UK/USA

Swamp Cypress UK/USA

Large, deciduous conifer grown for its water-loving character and beautiful autumn colour. It has special stems or roots that allow it to grow in shallow water.

Soil and situation: wet conditions in sun or shade.

Design notes: an excellent choice for wet to swampy ground.

 25 m (80 ft) ↔ 15 m (50 ft)

Veronicastrum virginicum '**Fascination**'

Brooklime UK/USA

Water-loving, spreading plant with thin, green leaves and spire-shaped clusters of brilliant blue flowers.

Soil and situation: deep, rich, moist soil or water to a depth of 15 cm (6 in) in a sunny situation.

Design notes: a good choice for a small, natural pond or for the watery edges of a bog garden. The deep blue colour of the flowers look particularly fine when set against a backdrop of dark green foliage.

↕ 10 cm (4 in) ↔ indefinite

OTHER BACKDROP PLANTS

- *Acer* **spp. (Maples):** delicate trees grown mostly for their colour; they look perfect alongside water.
- *Cardamine pratensis* **(Cuckoo Flower):** a meadow plant with cress-like leaves and small, lilac-blue flowers – good for a damp meadow.
- *Dodecatheon* **spp.:** delicate moisture-loving plants that like shade – a fine choice for a woodland water garden or a pond or meadow.
- *Eucalyptus* **spp.:** trees or shrubs grown for their colour and scent. Some species prefer boggy ground.
- *Phalaris arundinacea* var. *picta*: perennial grass with white and green striped leaves and white flowers – excellent for a cool green theme.
- *Vaccinium macrocarpon* **(Cranberry):** evergreen shrub with dark green leaves, pink flowers and red fruits – a good option for a bog garden.
- *Zizania aquatica* **(Canadian Wild Rice):** tall grass with flat leaves and delicate, pale green flowerheads. A lovely choice for a wildlife garden.

Fish and other fauna

Depending on the quality of the water, your pond will support just about anything that swims, hops, wriggles, crawls and flies, from fish and frogs to snails, newts and gnats. The wonderful thing about a water garden is that it is almost impossible to hold back the wildlife. The difficulty comes in achieving a balance between the different species. A good idea with a small pond is to introduce a few native fish, and see how they thrive, before going any further.

Left: If you particularly want to keep exhibition-grade fish such as the giant Koi carp, you should talk to a fish specialist before building your pond. Working in this way, you will be able to meet all their needs.

Below: Before introducing any fish, it is best to leave the pond for a year or so, letting other creatures such as frogs move in and establish themselves.

FISH FOR YOUR WATER GARDEN

Size and habitat are everything when you are trying to establish a fish pond. If the pond is too small and the fish too large in size and/or number, the fish will run into trouble. Some fish like clear, shallow water, while others like the water to be deep and murky. There are many other factors too – water temperature, moving water versus still water, winter conditions, sunlight and shade, this food versus that, and so on. The best way for beginners is to leave the pond for a year or so until the frogs, toads, newts, gnats, snails and all the other fauna take up residence, and then introduce a few native fish and see how they go. In an established wildlife pond, complete with a range of plants and fauna, fish will live quite happily on a mix of plants, insects and detritus. In an ornamental pond – where the water is clear with few or no plants – you will have to supply food. Alongside your very best trial-and-error efforts, you will soon find that natural selection and nature will sort things out.

Frequently asked questions

- **Are all goldfish gold?** No, they range from gold through to yellow-cream, with all sorts of black and brown markings. Some so-called goldfish are in fact Shubunkins.

- **Are the fish going to be happy with the fountain?** Some fish dislike moving water while others are happy – it depends on the species.

- **Are the fish going to get sucked into the pump?** Adult fish are fine, but eggs and fry do risk getting sucked through the pump. The same goes for frogspawn and tadpoles. The bigger the pond, the smaller the risk.

- **Are the fish going to breed?** If there is room and the fish are happy, established and the right size, they will breed.

- **Are the fish happy with underwater lighting?** It is fine if the pond is large enough to allow the fish to swim away into dark corners, but otherwise they are going to be traumatized. Do not leave the lights on all night.

- **Can I have big and small fish in the same pond?** Yes you can, but you have to be mindful that big, aggressive fish like tench are going to eat anything that comes their way. Again, the bigger the pond, the smaller the risk.

Roach

Characteristics ~ An attractive, reliable, subtly coloured fish, good for large, muddy-bottomed wildlife ponds and lakes. Colours range from yellow-red to brown-gold. Grows up to 25 cm (10 in) long and lives for 5–8 years.

Special note ~ A fish that will tolerate both clear and muddy water.

Rudd

Characteristics ~ A fat-bodied fish, suitable for both small and large ponds. Colours range from golden yellow to orange-red. Grows up to 30 cm (12 in) long and lives for 6–8 years.

Special note ~ A tough fish that will tolerate cloudy water, poor oxygen levels and big changes in temperature.

Koi

Characteristics ~ An exotic fish for both filtered ponds and large wildlife ponds. Colours range from yellow and black to white and red. Grows to 50–90 cm (20–36 in) long and lives for 50–100 years.

Special note ~ Koi are beautiful, but expensive and difficult to maintain. Think carefully before taking them on.

Common goldfish

Characteristics ~ A reliable fish, good for ponds in a cold climate. Colours range from reddish-gold to creamy yellow. Grows up to 40 cm (16 in) long and lives for 19–25 years.

Special note ~ Avoid fancy breeds of goldfish – they are more expensive, need more space, and are liable to perish in a cold winter.

Tench

Characteristics ~ A reliable, rather shy but aggressive fish, which might well eat small fry and tadpoles. Colours range from green to a pale orange-gold. Grows up to 40 cm (16 in) long and lives for 10–12 years.

Special note ~ A good idea for a large wildlife pond, but a bad idea if you want ornamental fish.

Common minnow

Characteristics ~ A swift-swimming tiddler, good for small wildlife ponds. Colours range from pale orange to silvery red-brown. Grows up to 8 cm (3½ in) long and lives for 2–5 years.

Special note ~ Shoals of minnows look wonderful in ponds and streams, and are loved by small children.

OTHER POND FAUNA

As well as teeming with microscopic life, a new pond will soon be alive with everything from frogs and newts to dragonflies and snails. Too many bugs can be a problem – they can damage the plants – but they soon (for the most part) become dinner for the other animals. If you observe that there are too many of one species, either remove them or encourage animals that find them tasty prey into the pond.

Frog

Dragonfly

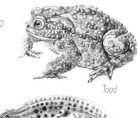
Toad

Snail

Water boatman

Newt

Stocking and care of fish

*How many
fish can I
have?*

Although much depends upon the size and depth of the pond and the water quality, as a general guide you can have 2.5 cm (1 in) of fish length for every hand-sized area of water surface. That said, as fish numbers are self-regulating – if there are too many, the fish won't breed and/or diseases and parasites will thin them out – it is best to introduce small numbers of fish and see what happens. You cannot go wrong if you put in just one or two at a time.

STOCKING YOUR POND

Type The best way to start is with a few fish that are long-established or native to your area; these might include goldfish, rudd, tench, stickleback, minnow or carp. Look at your pond or pool, consider the needs of the various species, and then stock your pond accordingly. Be aware that some fish are aggressive – they may even eat other fish.

Size Look for fish that are not much bigger than about 7.5–15 cm (3–6 in) in total length. Big fish not only cost more, but they will also be more difficult to transport and more likely to have difficulties settling down.

Getting the fish home If you get your fish from a specialist supplier, they will put them in a plastic bag with a small amount of air for the journey. Sit the bag in the car in a nice cool place, and get the fish home in the shortest possible time. If the fish are large and expensive, get the supplier to be responsible for the transportation.

Introducing fish to the pond When you get them home, undo the bag and sit it in the shallows at the side of the pond. Watch out for cats! After about an hour, gently ease the bag over so that the fish can quietly swim out into the pond.

Specific fish need specific conditions. Always ask a fish specialist for advice before making any choices or purchases.

Quantity guide

As a very rough guide, your pond will support 2.5 cm (1 in) of fish length for each 30 cm² (1 sq ft) of water surface – or you could say about 9 little goldfish for each 1 m² (1 sq yd).

1 x 2 m pond (= 2 m²)
Approximately 18 small goldfish. This figure is based on the fact that some fish will both grow in size and breed, while others will die.

2 x 2 m pond (= 4 m²)
Approximately 36 small goldfish. If you decide to have a mix of species, say small goldfish and larger tench, you will have to adjust the numbers accordingly.

4 x 2 m pond (= 8 m²)
While a pond of this size will in theory support approximately 72 small goldfish, you have to be aware that a healthy population will always be in a state of change, with fish breeding, growing in size and dying.

TOP FISH-BUYING TIPS

- Choose a reputable specialist – ideally one that has been personally recommended.

- Each fish tank in the shop should be fitted with its own filtered water supply, so as to contain and avoid disease.

- You should be able to choose precisely the fish you want.

- Look for a fish that has bright clear eyes, an upright top fin, and unblemished skin.

- Avoid fish with missing scales, torn fins and white spots on the body.

- Go for small, lively fish.

- The fish should be scooped up with a soft plastic net – with the minimum of trauma.

- The fish should be handed over in a plastic bag – half-full of water and pumped up with air/oxygen.

- Avoid transporting the fish in very hot or very cold weather.

FEEDING

In an established wildlife pond, one with a good range of plants growing in, outside and near the water, the fish will be able to feed quite happily on water insects, flying insects, pond plants and detritus from the bottom of the pond. In an ornamental pond, where the bottom is clear and there are few or no plants, you will need to feed the fish on good-quality prepacked fish food – things like dried flies, shredded shrimps and ant eggs. Feed them at the same time every day, say about midday when the temperature of the water has risen. Give them slightly too little rather than slightly too much. A good tip is to watch the fish feeding and only give them what they can eat in the space of around 3–4 minutes. Try to avoid a situation where scraps get left over, as a build-up of stale food will pollute the water. You don't have to feed in the winter when the fish are in a semi-dormant state and are able to live on their own body fat.

ROUTINE TASKS

Apart from giving the fish additional food, and generally making sure the water is clean and healthy-looking, you need to establish a regular care programme. Inspect the fish to make sure that they look healthy, with no unusual behaviour or strange skin discolorations. If you see a fish semi-floating, or in a very still or torpid condition, use a soft net to scoop it out of the pond. Keep it in an isolation tank. Try, when you are netting the fish, to guide it into a bowl of water, rather than lifting it clear of the water. Be mindful that breeding fish sometimes roll about in the warm shallows. Also check that the pond is not becoming overrun with any one type of flora or fauna, such as too many snails, algae or duckweed. Make sure in very hot weather that the water is at the correct level. If and when you clean out the pond, be careful that you do not damage any small fish that are hidden away in the mud.

FISH TROUBLESHOOTING

Overcrowding If the pond is overstocked, the fish will demonstrate the fact by eating each other, failing to breed or becoming ill. To a great extent, the problem should be self-regulating.

Predators Some big fish will eat some little fish, cats eat fish, some water snakes eat fish, birds such as herons eat fish, some mammals such as rats and stoats eat fish, and so on. The best you can do is avoid putting the wrong fish together, and to watch out for birds and cats. The other red-in-tooth-and-claw behaviour is simply part of the great plan and should be observed as such.

Freezing In winter, leave a large floating ball in the water so that there is always a hole in the ice. Never hit the ice, because this can traumatize the fish. Some species need to be brought indoors over winter.

Death Do fish feel pain? Dead fish are best removed from the water, as they might have an infectious disease. As for a dying fish, fishermen give them a well-placed blow on the head. If in doubt, consult a specialist vet.

Boredom Can a fish become bored? Avoid the situation by keeping them in a wildlife pond with plenty of plants, mud and refuge.

Overexcitement Fish get overexcited because it is feeding time, they are afraid of predators, there is not enough oxygen in the water or it is time for breeding. The best you can do is to feed them correctly, try to keep predators away and to ensure that the water is well oxygenated.

Lice

Symptoms The lice are clearly visible hanging on the body of the fish. Badly affected fish will die.

Treatment Use a small paintbrush carefully to dab the lice, first with paraffin and then with a special fish antiseptic.

White spot

Symptoms These parasites look like minute grains of sand. Infected fish will be seen rubbing against the side of the pool.

Treatment Depending upon the size of the pond, treatment involves using a proprietary cure either in the pond itself or in an isolation tank.

Ulcer

Symptoms The disease presents itself variously as bloody spots, rotting fins and blotchy swellings.

Treatment Although it can be treated in the very early stages, the disease is so rampant that it is best to remove and destroy affected fish.

Fungus

Symptoms There are several types of fungus, the most common being mouth fungus and cotton wool fungus.

Treatment Remove affected fish and put them in an isolation tank. Treat them with a proprietary medication. Consult a specialist vet.

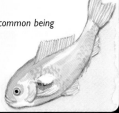

Looking after water gardens

General maintenance of a water garden is not so much difficult as ongoing. You will have to sort out the ponds and water features, perhaps persuade troublesome toads to go away, and generally keep an eye on the fish and fauna around the garden. These watery tasks apart, however, the maintenance involves much the same jobs as with any garden: mowing any grass areas, mending items, pruning shrubs and trees, mulching, looking after paths and walls, and so on.

Routine tasks

Spring
Clean out the pond, carry out repairs, put pumps and fountains back in place (see page 71), tend and replace plants, and generally make good anything that sustained winter damage, such as fence and gate posts.

Begin to bring out furniture as the weather permits. Check on bird boxes.

Summer
Take a close look at ponds and water features every week (see page 70). Some pondweed-type plants are so prolific that they need to be generally skimmed and removed from the water.

Apart from the water-related tasks, you will also have to mow lawns, rake gravel, tidy up borders, and generally keep all the waterside plants under control.

Autumn
Clean up dead leaves and debris, trim back dying foliage, divide plants, and remove delicate plants for overwintering. Be very careful when cleaning a butyl/plastic-lined pond that you do not damage the liner – no spikes, sharp sticks and garden forks (see also page 71). This is a real problem when you have created a really successful wildlife pond, because it is easy to forget that there is a lining that can be damaged.

Make running repairs to items like gates, walls and pergolas. Secure loose flapping items that might be a problem in the winter. Check that fence panels are strong and stable.

In a wildlife water garden, leave piles of logs, bags of dead leaves, upturned flower pots and stacks of bricks at various positions around the garden, so that there are places for birds and small animals like frogs, toads, newts and mice to shelter. If you want to encourage larger animals like hedgehogs and badgers to come in, then construct underground shelters.

Winter
Remove the last dead leaves from around the garden. Wash all the structures with warm water – sides of formal ponds, tiles, brickwork, paving, pondside furniture, anything that looks grubby. Put things like furniture away for the winter.

In a wildlife water garden, put food like fat and nuts out for the birds. Some people drain formal ponds.

Troubleshooting

See also pages 76–77.

Falling water level
If the water level is falling fast, first find a home for the fish and plants, and then drain the pond in order to assess and correct the problem (see page 73).

Distressed fish
If the fish are gasping for air in hot weather, first top the pond up with a hose, and then fit a large pump with a spray fountain to oxygenate the water (see page 71).

Pump failure
If the pump stops working, check the power supply, and then switch off the pump. Remove the pump and clean it thoroughly (see page 71). Consider having a back-up pump.

MAINTENANCE OF HARD MATERIALS

Brickwork
Scrub and wash brickwork in early spring. Small areas of damaged coursework, on garden walls and patios, can be repointed with a weak cement and sand mix.

Stonework
Apart from washing green and slimy steps, real stone is best left to develop a patina. Old joints need to be swept clean and repaired with a weak mortar mix of 1 part cement, 6 parts soft sand and 1 part lime.

Decking patios
A well-built and maintained wooden deck will last about 25 years. The biggest danger is damp. The best defence is to clean up debris so that the wood can dry out in the sun and wind. Moulds and wood-eating insects do not do so well if the wood is crisp and dry.

Gates and fences
A well-built and maintained gate complete with posts will last about 25 years – especially if the wood has been pressure-treated. Wooden fence panels should last a good ten years or more. The biggest dangers to gates and fences are damp and wind damage. Clean away the debris from around posts, and make sure they are well secured in readiness for winter.

GENERAL PRUNING

Pruning is defined as the removal of parts of a woody plant in order to shape and train it, maintain its good health, achieve a balance between growth and flowering, and improve the quality of fruit, flowers, leaves and stems that it produces.

Trees Established trees need little pruning. You only need prune if too many branches overhang the pond, the roots of say a bamboo seem to be heading for the plastic liner of a pond, or the branches are dying.

Shrubs For many flowering shrubs, yearly pruning is needed to encourage the development of the flowers. Early-flowering shrubs are pruned as soon as the flowers fade. Late summer-flowering shrubs are pruned during the following late spring. Winter-flowering shrubs need little pruning other than to cut out congested and damaged stems. Some shrubs have very vigorous root systems. If you ever see roots heading for liner ponds, then either move the shrubs, or root-prune them.

Climbers Climbers need little regular pruning, other than to cut back old and tangled woody stems. In this instance, half the old stems are cut out in the first year, and the other half in the second year when new stems are established.

Hedges For a foliage hedge, in the first year the young plants are cut back to half their height, and in the second year the hedge is cut back four times between early spring and late summer. For a spring-flowering hedge, the plants can be pruned as soon as the flowers fade in early summer. For a summer-flowering hedge, the pruning is done in the following spring.

Roses Established bush roses planted in autumn and winter are pruned in early spring before the leaves appear. Prune miniature roses in autumn or late winter. A newly planted rose hedge is pruned hard back in the early spring of the first year, less severely in the late winter of the second year, and slightly in the winter of following years.

THE WATER GARDENER'S PLANT-CARE CALENDAR

Spring
- **Waterside plants** Prune shrubs, prepare soil, plant out selected beds, and generally tidy up after the winter.
- **Bog and moisture-loving plants** Thin out some plants and replace others. Buy plants like irises and reeds. Consider extending the area of planting.
- **Emergents** Overgrown plants can be lifted and divided. Now is the time to add extra plants.
- **Floating-leaf plants** Buy new plants, such as waterlilies, and put them in place in the pond.
- **Aquatics** Bring out plants that have been overwintered indoors, and perhaps buy new plants.

Summer
- **Backdrop plants** Plant bedding plants, train climbers, plant out pot-grown plants, and prune climbing plants and shrubs to encourage new growth. Harvest vegetables and selected fruit. Clip and mow lawns. Support plants as and when the need arises.
- **Bog and moisture-loving plants** Check that the soil is moist without being flooded. Support tall plants such as *Zantedeschia aethiopica* (Arum Lily). Deadhead plants as needed, and remove damaged leaves.
- **Emergents** Cut back and tidy up plants if they fall over and start to rot in the water.
- **Floating-leaf plants** Aim to have about two-thirds of the water surface covered in some sort of foliage.
- **Aquatics** Make sure that plants like *Lemna* (Duckweed) and *Ranunculus aquatilis* (Water Buttercup) do not run out of control. You might need to cut back some of the more rampant species.

Autumn
- **Backdrop plants** Cut back overgrown plants, support plants, and generally clean up leaves and debris.
- **Bog and moisture-loving plants** Lift and divide plants that are out of control. Remove dead and dying foliage.
- **Emergents** Lift and divide plants that are crowding out smaller neighbours.
- **Floating-leaf plants** Remove dead foliage from the surface of the water.
- **Aquatics** Depending upon your area, some plants will need to be brought in for the winter.

Winter
- **Backdrop plants** Clean up debris and fork and mulch around the base of tender plants.
- **Bog and moisture-loving plants** Remove debris.
- **Emergents** Remove dead leaves and debris.
- **Floating-leaf plants** Leave well alone.
- **Aquatics** Check on plants that you have brought indoors.

Sometimes there comes a point when you have to remove plants for the greater good. Cut back any plants that threaten to take over.

Pond maintenance

Is this a messy task?

Y ou will have to clean pumps, make small repairs to structures, replace, divide and move plants, mend leaks, remove dead and dying fish, and so on, all of which will mean getting wet and dirty. The whole business of working with water, however, is uniquely exciting and therapeutic. So, when there is a wet and watery problem that needs fixing, just get in there and enjoy the fun! If children want to help – and they will – make sure you keep a close watch on them.

ROUTINE TASKS

Summer
Clean small pump filters once a week. Switch off the power, lift the pump from the pond, remove algae and debris, give the filter a wash in warm, soapy water, rinse in clear water, and fit and replace. Top the pond up with fresh water. On any hot muggy nights, run the fountain or hose spray to oxygenate the water.

Autumn
Clean out dead leaves and debris, trim back dying foliage, divide plants, and move delicate plants indoors for overwintering. You might have to remove the leaves 3–4 times over the autumn period.

Winter
Take out the last dead leaves, remove and clean pumps, filters and fountains, and place a large ball in the pond to break up the ice. Always switch the power off before touching the pump.

Spring
Clean out the pond, carry out repairs, put pumps and fountains back into position, and tend and replace plants. Wash small, formal ponds and water features in warm water.

CONTROLLING PLANT GROWTH

Backdrop plants If you look at a natural stream, lake or pond, you will see that there is a tendency for one or two species to dominate. For example, the side of a lake might be covered in willows and reeds and not much else. The challenge is to group plants together that are happy to grow in each other's shadow. You might have willows, various reeds, swathes of daffodils, or whatever you prefer. You could control the growth by mimicking traditional agriculture systems, by harvesting the reeds and pollarding the willows.

Bog and moisture-loving plants If you have a bog plant that is so successful that it is crowding out its neighbours – say one or more irises – you have a choice. You can let it get on with it, create a separate bog area for other species, or divide and lift plants to make space for new plants. Alternatively, enjoy the fact that irises do so well by taking up the challenge and introducing a whole range with different colours, sizes and flowering periods.

Emergents Unwanted emergent plants can be divided and lifted in the autumn. Be aware that some, like *Typha minima* (Common Reedmace), send out very sharp, pointed roots, which are strong enough to pierce a bare foot or flexible liner. A good idea with a small, natural pond is to plant emergents in baskets, so that you can lift them out and act accordingly – dividing, root pruning or whatever is appropriate.

Floating-leaf plants A successful natural pond needs at least two-thirds of the water surface to be covered in foliage. Too little and the sunlight encourages plants like algae to grow out of control; too much and the dark water will result in an imbalance in the fish and fauna. Remove any excess growth.

Aquatics Sometimes, especially in new ponds, one of the aquatic plants will become rampant. If this happens, you should keep removing unwanted growth until one of the other species becomes well established.

CARE OF FISH

Apart from food, fish need good-quality water and just the right amount of space (see page 66 for the fish-to-water ratio). If you misjudge one or other of these needs, the fish will suffer. The water does not necessarily need to be clear, but it does need to be sweet-smelling. Good fish care starts with careful observation. Check the pond every day or so. If the fish are torpid or patched with white, or the water smells like a drain or is covered with a thin layer of green slime, then there are problems (see page 67). When you are thinking of introducing new fish, make sure that you get them from a recommended specialist.

Restocking

Think carefully before adding new fish. You do not want too many fish, or fish that are going to fight with each other, and you do not want to introduce diseases (see pages 66–67).

Pond repairs

If the water level starts dropping, kit yourself out with some old clothes and prepare yourself for action (see page 73). This is especially important if the pond is packed full of fish.

WHEN AND HOW TO CLEAN THE POND

Depending upon the size, type and condition of your pond, cleaning will involve some part of the following procedures. The good news is that big natural wildlife ponds rarely need cleaning, other than to divide plants.

- In late autumn or very early spring, gently pump most of the water onto a neighbouring bed or border.
- As you go, very carefully net the fish and put them into holding buckets and tanks.
- Remove containerized plants (those which are growing in baskets and pots).
- Switch off, remove and clean the pump.
- Remove floating-leaf plants and aquatics/oxygenators.
- Scoop out the rest of the water.
- Remove the mud and put it on waterside beds and borders, so that the small creatures can make their way back to the water. Keep a small amount of the mud in a bucket. You could help out creatures like snails, newts, bugs and beetles by putting them in the bucket of mud.
- Brush and clean the pond, and check for potential structural problems.
- Wash and clean small, formal ponds with warm water.
- Divide and replace plants to suit.
- Partially refill the pond, and replace the containerized plants and the bucket of mud. Slide the mud slowly into place, to avoid clouding the water.
- Refill the pond with water and then replace all the remaining plants.
- Carefully return all the fish to the water.

MAINTENANCE CHECKLIST

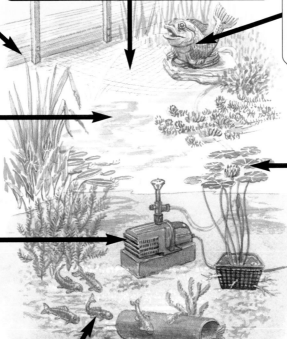

Structures

Inspect structures such as bridges, decking and brickwork, and make any necessary repairs.

Netting

Nothing looks worse than a saggy, baggy net draped over a pond. It might catch a few leaves, but it will not keep off cats, birds and children. Use stretched wires and fences.

Fountains

Fountains look good, and they oxygenate the water, but only when they are working. Feeble, dead and dying fountains need to be removed, or cleaned and restored to good order. Replace kinked or blocked pipes, and reset valves and taps.

Weed

Green, slime-type weeds can be twirled around a stick and flicked onto the neighbouring border or bed, or into the compost heap – kids love this! Remove wildlife from the weed and replace in the pond.

Plants

For a good, eco-friendly pond, about two-thirds of the water surface should be covered in foliage. Remove excess foliage or add new plants as necessary. Thin out any other plants that are growing out of control. Most can be simply cut or sliced in half and replanted.

Pump

Turn off the power and remove the pump from the pond. Wash the whole mechanism in warm water. Clean small pumps at more frequent intervals.

Winter precautions

Make a decision about semi-hardy plants: either let them take their chance, or put them in containers and bring them indoors.

Delicate floating plants must be brought indoors.

Fish

Look at the fish. If they are so sluggish that you can easily catch them with a net, take a close look at them to make sure they are free from white splotches or patches. Remove any suspect fish.

Make sure that there is adequate shelter for the fish. Put clay pots and pipes into the water – anything to give fish and pondlife good cover and protection.

Water-garden repairs

Is it easy to repair a leak?

Although repairs to general structures such as fences, gates, walls, paths and patios are much the same as with any other garden, the real difficulty with water gardens comes when there is a pond-related problem that just cannot be ignored. The good news for the water gardener is that the mere notion of ponds leaking, and lots of fish and wildlife needing to be rescued, is usually so exciting that friends and family are likely to offer copious amounts of help.

REPAIRING CONCRETE PAVING

If, when you are cleaning the paving, you notice that a slab is cracked or broken, it is a good idea to put it right before it upsets neighbouring slabs, or before you trip over. Clean the moss and weeds out from around the slab, take measurements, and find a replacement. If it is an old slab, with odd measurements, an odd texture or a strange colour, the best option is to try an architectural salvage yard.

Break the damaged slab with a hammer; then use an old chisel to ease the fragments clear and to clean out all traces of hard mortar. Line the recess with a bed of fresh sand or with five blobs of new mortar. Encircle the new slab with two slings made from fine, strong twine, and gently lower it into place. The twine will enable you to repeatedly lift and lower the slab without doing damage to your back, your fingertips and/or neighbouring slabs. Make small adjustments to the sand/mortar thickness under the slab until it is at the correct level. Finally, cut and remove the twine and fill the joints to match the original.

REPAIRING BLOCK PAVING

Establish exactly how many damaged pavers need to be replaced, and try to search out new ones that will match the originals. If the pavers are unusual in any way, then architectural salvage yards are often a good source. Use a hammer and chisel to break and remove the damaged pavers. Set the new pavers in place, all nicely bedded and levelled on a layer of dry fine sand. Use a rubber mallet to gently ease and tap the pavers into place. Finally, shake dry silver sand down into the joint.

REPAIRING OLD BRICK PAVING

If the bricks are old and bedded on traditional lime mortar, ease the broken bricks clear and then use the fragments to search out well-matching replacements. Be aware that old pavings and patios sometimes used high-fired house bricks with the 'frog' positioned on the underside. Use a hammer and chisel to clear away the old mortar. Mix up a small amount of new mortar to a soft but slightly stiff consistency (1 part cement, 6 parts soft sand, 1 part lime) and bed the new bricks in place. Be careful not to put so much mortar in the recess that it oozes up and out of the joints. Finally, use the mortar to point the joints. You can also give the new mortar a slightly weathered look by wiping it over with a cloth or a soft brush.

REPAIRING BRICKWORK

Isolated bricks within a garden wall may become frost-damaged and start to crumble; this condition occurs with poor-grade bricks and is known as 'spalling'. Find new, matching bricks, and use a brick chisel and hammer to cut out the damaged bricks. Be careful not to damage the surrounding wall by trying to lever the bricks out. Chisel out all the old mortar from the recesses and brush out the dust. Working with one brick at a time, dampen the new brick and the interior of the recess, line the bottom, sides and back of the recess with a slightly stiff mortar, and lastly butter the top of the brick with mortar and ease it into place. Finally, repoint the joints. If the weather is very hot and dry, then spray both bricks and wall with water.

REPOINTING

Sculpt wide joints to a good finish.

Repointing is a process of replacing old mortar. Use a hammer, chisel and brush to clean out the old mortar. Spread a stiff, creamy pancake of mortar over a piece of plywood to match the thickness of the joint to be repointed. Cut one edge of the mortar pancake to a straight edge. Take the small trowel and cut a slice off the straight edge of the mortar, so that you finish up with a strip of new mortar on the back edge of the trowel. Wipe the strip of mortar into the joint to be filled. Finally when the joint is full and the mortar is nearly dry, use the point of the trowel or a piece of old, dry rag to shape and texture the new pointing so that it looks like the original.

REPAIRING BROKEN FENCE POSTS

Set the new post in rubble and concrete.

Remove the stub of old post along with any concrete or metal fixing. Dig the hole out to a depth of 40 cm (16 in). Put a tile or brick in the hole and set the new post in place. Tap a small amount of rubble around the bottom of the post and use battens set at an angle to prop up the post. Make adjustments and check with a spirit (carpenter's) level. Fill the hole with a concrete mix of 1 part cement, 2 parts sharp sand and 3 parts coarse aggregate (gravel).

REPLACING FENCE PANELS

Remove foliage and such like, so that you can move freely around the fence. Remove the broken panel complete with old fixings. Position the new panel between the posts and prop it up at the correct level (see right). Clamp the panel in place. Drill holes through the edges of the panel – into the posts – and screw it in place with galvanized screws, and/or use new galvanized fixings.

POND REPAIRS

Raised, rigid-liner ponds

The most common problem with raised, rigid-liner ponds is that sand that has been poured into the cavity between the liner and the outside wall sinks, with the effect that the liner sags and threatens to crack and/or lever off the coping slabs. Empty the pond, remove the coping slabs and, with the help of a friend, work systematically around the pond easing and lifting the liner while at the same time pouring fresh, dry sand into the cavity. Once the base and sides of the liner are supported, simply replace the coping slabs.

Edges of a raised brick pond

The most common problem with raised brick ponds is that, with the walls only being about 10 cm (4 in) thick, the coping slabs about 30 cm (1 ft) square, and the slabs being centred on the walls so that there is an overhang of about 10 cm (4 in) at each side, the coping is inherently unstable. The moment someone leans on the coping it levers itself off. The answer is to build a second brick wall around the first, so that you finish up with a double wall about 20 cm (8 in) thick, with the 30 cm (1 ft) coping slabs only over-hanging by 5 cm (2 in) at each side. The finished coping will easily be strong enough to take your weight.

Flexible liners

If a flexible liner starts to leak, the first thing to do is find a temporary home for the fish and plants. Once the way is clear, drain the pond and search around for the leak. This will be no problem if you caused the leak with something like a spike, but if the whole thing is a mystery it will not be so easy. The liner is also likely to be muddy or slimy or both, so it is quite a problem. If you are lucky, you will spot a root or stone pushing up through the liner, or bubbles coming up through the mud.

The repair procedures are much the same with butyl and PVC, the only difference being that you must use compatible solvents and tape. Once the leak has been identified, remove the cause and clean and dry the whole area around the leak – so that there is an all-round clean area of at least 30 cm (1 ft).

Having cleaned, dried and polished the area, wipe it over with petroleum (WARNING: put the petrol (gas) well out of the way the moment you have finished with it).

Make a patch of new liner to fit the prepared area. Set double-sided rubber tape on the liner, remove the waxed backing paper, set the patch in place, and then use an electric (power) paint-stripper to warm the patch while you are applying pressure. If the mend is in a flat area, cover it with another sheet of butyl/PVC, and weigh it down with a concrete slab. Finally, fill up the pond with water and the job is done.

Paving around a sunken pond

The most common problem with the paved edgings around sunken ponds is that they are overhanging the edge of the water with little or nothing to support them. Remove the slabs, dig a shallow trench around the circumference and top it up with concrete. Finally, set the slabs in place so that they are overhanging the water while being canted back at a slight angle.

Edges of a natural pond

The most common problem with natural ponds is that the edges are badly constructed. Having emptied the pond, pull the edge of the liner in towards the pond. Dig a trench around the edge and top it up with concrete. Pull the edge of the liner back over the concrete and build a mini brick wall that sits on the liner. Pull the edge of the liner up the outside of the wall, and flap it over so that it is looking towards the pond. Pack the earth at both sides of the wall, so that the wall is completely buried and on the inside of the pond. The edge of the pond will now be supported, while the edge of the liner is hidden from view.

Concrete ponds

Concrete ponds are prone to cracking. Although you can cut out the crack and try to make repairs, the easiest option is to line the whole structure with a top-quality PVC liner. Empty the pond and clean it out. Make sure that the concrete surface is free from anything sharp that is likely to damage the liner. Spread a blanket of geotextile over the inside of the pond, followed by the PVC liner. Make good the pond edges, as with any other pond, and fill it with water.

Pipes and cables

The most common problem with pipes and cables is that they get kinked, stretched and broken. The easiest solution is to enclose the pipes and cables in ducting. While you can enter the ducting through the 'wall' of a pond, through a rigid or flexible liner, using various glands and fixings, by far the easiest option is to run the ducting over the edge of the pond and then hide it with a pot, shrub piece of pretend grass matting, turf or whatever seems appropriate.

Developing a water garden

*How can I
improve my
water garden?*

Carefully study the garden. Take note of the structures, the way the pond is built, the type of materials used, the quality of the pumps and such like, and then try to come up with improvements that use what you have to best advantage. For example, do not dig up a small but well-built pond, but build a stream and waterfall, using the pond as the reservoir or the header pool. If you have moved into a new home, live with it for a year before making changes.

A water garden that has been well planned and developed will give pleasure both in the making and in the viewing, and it should also be a delight for generations to come.

Key areas for development

- You could make changes to an existing pond by turning it into a bog garden, by using it as a reservoir pool for a much larger feature, or by building a second pond at a different level to the first.

- You could unify loosely defined areas by linking them with lawns, beds or patios.

- You could change and modify the planting, and the shape and form of the structures, so that they all relate to a common theme – such as a Japanese water garden.

- You could link a series of small, separate ponds with a meandering stream.

- You could lower the height of the backdrop planting to create sunnier areas.

- You could cover ugly existing concrete paths and patios with an instant surface such as gravel or crushed bark.

- You could partially cover an overly large pond with a structure like a bridge, jetty, pier or deck.

DEVELOPING AN ECOSYSTEM

The ecosystem of a pond is best defined as a healthy natural state of affairs where all the elements that go to make up the pond – sunlight, rain, earth, plants, animals, minute pond organisms and yourself – are all part of a cyclical interaction that makes for a well-balanced holistic totality. Every element, or you might say all parties, both give and take from the system.

You hold the key that sets the system in motion. If you provide good clean water, the wheel will start to turn. The sunlight encourages the growth of algae, and the algae will provide a breeding ground for small creatures. Fish and wildlife feed on the algae and small creatures, and in so doing produce waste matter that falls in the water. Dead and dying plants fall alongside the waste matter to form detritus. Floating-leaf pond plants limit the sunlight so that there are not too many fish and algae. Large birds eat the frogs and wildlife that come in to eat the fish and plants. Flying insects both feed on the detritus and are eaten by the pondlife. Birds

and frogs feed on the insects. Dead and dying animals and insects fall to the bottom of the pond to form organic matter for plant growth. The sunlight causes green plants to take up carbon dioxide and give off oxygen, which in turn helps to maintain clean water … and so the wheel goes round.

You can help the system along by being tolerant. If you want the birds and fish, you have to settle for the gnats and a slightly soupy water. You can have waterlilies and the like, but you must not let them grow out of control to the detriment of other plants. You can have fish, but along with the fish you have to settle for having hunters that eat fish – herons, water snakes, frogs, small mammals and cats. Much the same goes for all the slugs, mice, crows and other beasts that you might think of as being pests; they all play their part. You must be aware that if you, for example, poison slugs and spray roses, then you risk, at the other end of the wheel, killing off your favourite fish. Your challenge is to try to keep the whole system in carefully balanced motion.

DEVELOPMENT EXAMPLES

The best water gardens are ones that are in a constant state of flux. A small improvement to a plant, path, texture or structure can dramatically change a garden. One way to proceed is to draw up a master plan that can be developed in stages or phases. So, for example, the pond could be built and developed in one year, extra trees planted in the next year, a stream added the next, and so on. Be aware that a water garden can turn into a lifetime's project.

BEFORE

Here there are too many trees overlooking the pond, and the circular wall of the raised pond is rather grim and overpowering.

AFTER

The hedge has been reshaped, the large trees have been removed and the edge of the pond has been remodelled to soften it with planting.

This square pond has been changed by removing the harsh edging stones, and then creating planting beds and a bog garden that blur the line between land and water.

This circular pond has been developed by removing the edging stones, and then creating a 'beach' with sand, shingle, dry planting and an octagonal deck.

RESHAPING PONDS

Existing ponds cannot easily be reshaped. Certainly, you can remove the flexible liner from a small pond, and dig a bigger hole and fit a new liner, but that constitutes a complete change rather than a reshape. A better idea would be to build a second pond alongside the first, so that the narrow strip of land between the two becomes a dynamic bridge-like feature that appears to cross over a large pond.

You can increase the apparent size of a natural pond by building bog gardens around its edges, and planting bog plants that are happy to grow both in wet soil and in shallow water. The planting will fool the eye into thinking that the pond and the bog gardens are a single, much larger feature.

WHEN BETTER LEFT ALONE

An old natural pond or stream, meaning a long-standing part of the landscape, is usually best left alone. You can build small additions like paths and bog gardens, but for the most part it is wise not to change the waterside planting or anything that might upset the existing ecosystem.

Additions to consider

• A second pond at a different level

• A bridge or pier crossing an existing pond

• A duck house complete with ducks

• A stylish fountain to change the character

• A waterfall to give more drama

• A fence to create a private area

• A change in planting to create a focal point

• A change to a slope to create terracing and steps

• A patio along a pond

• A pergola to create an eye-catching feature

Troubleshooting

Why won't it work?

Digging holes, building walls, fitting pumps, planting and generally playing around with mud and water – creating a water garden is a wonderfully exciting, skill-stretching, life-enhancing challenge. There are always going to be hitches along the way, however. You have switched on the pump, and … nothing! The wall-mask spout delivers no more than a dribble, and it just does not work. What do you do? This is where we start to sort out some common problems.

WATER-GARDEN TROUBLESHOOTING

PROBLEM	LIKELY CAUSE	POSSIBLE SOLUTIONS
The water level in the pond is falling.	Damage to the pond lining.	Keep topping the pond up until the weather is good; then find a home for the plants and fish, drain the pond, and search out the leak and make a repair.
The pump is making sucking noises but no water comes out.	A kink or blockage in the pipe, or the filter is totally clogged.	Turn off power and remove the pump. Wash the filter and the body of the pump, make sure that all feed and delivery pipes are clear, and replace badly kinked pipes.
The pump sounds as if it is working but the fountain spray is feeble.	Pipes are blocked and/or the valves on the pump are blocked and/or badly set. The delivery pipe could be coming away from the fountain.	Make sure all pipes are clear, clean and well fitted. Wash the pump and filter, and reset the valves.
The goldfish have white blotches around the mouth and body.	Fish have a white-spot type of fungal disease.	Isolate the fish in a holding tank and treat them with proprietary medicine. The problem is indicative of poor water quality, poor food, too many fish and/or poor stock.
The fish gasp for air in warm weather.	Low oxygen levels in the water and/or the fish are breeding.	Turn on a fountain to oxygenate the water, increase the number of oxygenating plants, and generally keep an eye on the fish.
The fish are vanishing.	Predators.	Keep an eye on the pond. Watch out for cats, birds, rats, foxes, water snakes, children – anything that might take the fish – and then guard against the problem.
When the weather is warm, the fish roll about in the shallows.	Fish breed from spring through to summer; it could be that the females are laying eggs or the males fertilizing the eggs.	If the water looks in good condition, and the fish look healthy, just keep monitoring the problem.
Not many of the fish fry (baby fish) appear to survive.	Lack of oxygen or disease, or too many predators.	Turn on the fountain to oxygenate the water, increase oxygenating plants, top the pond up with clean water, remove scum from the surface of the water, scoop out dead fish. Make sure that the pond is not topped up with rainwater run-off from farmland. Make sure there are not too many water boatmen and other pond creatures that feed on young fish. Make sure the pump is not sucking the fish in. Be aware that, in the normal course of events, only a very small proportion of the fry survive.

WATER-GARDEN TROUBLESHOOTING

PROBLEM	LIKELY CAUSE	POSSIBLE SOLUTIONS
The newly introduced fish are rubbing themselves raw against structures within the pond.	Fish lice or other parasites.	Remove the fish and put them in a holding tank. Treat the fish with a proprietary medicinal bath. Next time, remember to get your fish from a different supplier.
The water is green with algae.	Too much sunlight resulting in an imbalance in the ecosystem within the pond.	Make sure that about two-thirds of the water surface is covered with floating-leaf plants, drop submerged oxygenating plants into the water, and spread a small amount of barley straw onto the water. Cut back waterside plants that hang over the water.
The pond plants are dying and there is an ammonia-like smell coming from the pond.	Poor-quality water, or possibly run-off of rainwater from chemically sprayed farmland.	Clean out the pond and change the water. Make sure that the pond is not topped up with rainwater from farmland.
The butyl liner is bulging up from the bottom of the pond.	Gas and/or water is trapped under the liner – a common problem in wet, low-lying land when there is a high water table.	If the problem will not go away, drain the pond and roll back the liner, dig a deep sump with a soakaway trench leading off to lower ground, fill it with rubble, cover it all with sand, and replace the liner. If the problem continues, you have the choice of fitting a pump in the sump, or moving the pond to higher ground.
There are bubbles of smelly gases coming up from the bottom of the pond.	Pond is too shallow, there is not enough oxygen in the water, the water is too warm, there is too much organic sludge.	Oxygenate the water with plants and a fountain, and make sure at least one-third of the water surface is free from plants. Cut back any plants that are dropping leaves and bits and pieces into the water. Remove some of the pond sludge.
The stone slabs on the patio area around a raised pond are sinking.	Poor drainage, water undermining the paving and/or a poor foundation.	Remove the paving, put down a 15 cm (6 in) layer of compacted rubble followed by a 5 cm (2 in) thick slab of concrete, and relay the slabs on blobs of mortar.
The irises are being eaten, almost to the point of extinction.	The likely culprit is the caterpillar stage of the iris sawfly.	Remove the caterpillars by hand. Bombard both the irises and the pests with a fine jet of water. Encourage the broadest range of wildlife into the garden, in the hope that some bird, beetle, frog or other creature will enjoy eating the sawflies.
Some of the plants around the pond are turning a spotty, yellow-brown colour.	The plants are probably under attack by leafhoppers.	Spray the plants with a jet from the hose, so as to knock the leafhoppers into the water, where they will be eaten by the fish.
As the water level rises in my flexible-liner wild pond it slowly trickles out on one side, with the effect that the garden is wet on the overflow side, and the liner is always on view on the other side.	Pond has been built on a slight tilt so that the low edge of the pond has become an overflow point – a common problem.	You have two choices: either build up the low side of the pond, so that the water level rises to hide all traces of the liner, or you can leave the pond as it is, and build bog gardens at the soggy overflow side, and plant a 'curtain' of emergent plants at the other side to hide the liner.

Glossary

Aggregate Loose mixture of pebbles crushed stone and sand in concrete; similar to ballast.

Algae Microscopic plants, mostly aquatic; in general terms, the green slime that forms on stagnant water.

Amphibious Describes creatures that live both on land and in water, such as frogs or newts.

Annuals Plants that live out their life (flower, set seed and die) in a single growing season.

Aquatic plants Plants that can grow either in water or with its roots in saturated ground.

Armoured cable Power cable that is protected with an additional covering.

Backfilling Filling a cavity, behind a wall or in a foundation trench hole, in order to bring the earth level up.

Bare-rooted Plants that are sold with bare roots, as opposed to container-grown plants that are sold with their roots in soil.

Biennials Plants that flower and die in the second growing season.

Bog garden Part of the garden, usually close to a pond, where the soil is permanently wet or damp.

Bog plants Plants that will grow with their roots in wet or damp soil. Because some plants will grow in anything from moist ground to shallow water, there is sometimes confusion between bog plants that enjoy very wet ground and emergent plants that enjoy growing in the outer margins of a pond.

Bonsai Art of growing miniaturized trees in containers.

Canal Straight channel that is obviously man-made.

Centring Setting a measurement or component part on the centre of another, or measuring a length or width to find the centre.

Compacting Using a hammer and/or the weight of your body to press down on a layer of sand, earth or hardcore.

Conduit Tube, pipe or duct enclosing and protecting power cables.

Coping Top course of a brick or stone wall, usually made of tiles, stone or bricks, usually sloped or angled for a decorative effect, and also to shed water.

Course Term used to describe the horizontal layers of brick or stone within a wall.

Curing time Time taken for mortar or concrete to become firm and stable. 'Part cured' means that the mortar or concrete is firm enough to take a small amount of weight.

Deciduous Describes plants that shed their leaves at the end of the growing season.

Delivery pipe Pipe at the output side of the pump, or a pipe or tap on the water-outlet end of a water system.

Emergent plants Plants that grow at the very edge of the pond, in shallow water and or in boggy soil. Suppliers sometimes have difficulties differentiating between plants that like very shallow water, and plants that like very wet soil. Also known as marginal plants.

Evergreen Describes plants that retain their leaves for more than one growing season.

Exotic plants Plants that are not native to temperate climates, and have a striking or unusual appearance.

Flexible liner Pond liner made from a flexible waterproof material such as butyl rubber or PVC.

Flow-adjustment valve Valve or tap on the delivery side of the pump that regulates or controls the rate of flow, commonly seen on fountain pumps.

Footing Shallow trench designed to carry a basic foundation of concrete.

Formwork See Shuttering.

Foundations Underground pads of concrete or compacted rubble that support the weight of paving, walls or other structures.

Frog Shallow depression or hollow on one side of a brick, designed as a key to hold the mortar.

Geotextile Purpose-made soft material, similar to carpet underlay, used to protect a flexible pond liner from sharp stones. See also Underlay.

Hardcore Mix of broken bricks and general builder's rubble, used to create a foundation; it is sorted to exclude items like plant material and wood, and then broken and compacted.

Hardy Describes a plant that is able to withstand year-round conditions, heavy frost, heavy rainfall and dry summers.

Head Maximum height that water is able to reach above an outlet, pump or reservoir pool.

Header pool Topmost pool or tank in a circulating water feature.

Levelling Using a spirit-level to decide whether or not a structure or component part is horizontally parallel to the ground, or vertically at right angles to the ground, and then going on to make adjustments to bring the component into line.

Marginal plants See Emergent plants.

Marking out Using items such as a pencil, rule, square, compass, pegs and string to mark out an area on the ground, in readiness for digging out, or otherwise taking the project forward.

Moisture-loving Describes plants that like growing in moist soil. Be aware of the tiny difference between bog plants that thrive in anything from damp soil through to very wet soil, and moisture-loving plants that thrive in well-drained but wet soil.

Mulch Covering of bark chippings, pebbles, sheet plastic, manure or other material applied in a layer over the soil in order to conserve moisture and cut back on weed growth.

Non-return valve One-way valve that allows water to flow in only one direction.

Oxygenators Oxygenating plants, also called aquatics and submerged plants, which release oxygen into the water. The foliage of such plants sometimes, but not always, breaks the surface of the water. In broad general terms, the foliage gives off bubbles of oxygen and the roots use up waste nutrients.

Perennials Plants, usually woody or herbaceous, that live for three or more seasons.

PVC Plastic material used for making small inexpensive water features and pipework that is both strong and durable.

Render Thin layer of mortar or cement spread as a thin sheet or layer, used to conceal or protect, such as a cement render over a concrete block wall.

Reservoir pool Tank or pool of water at the lowest point in a water circulating system, such as a reservoir pool at the bottom of a waterfall feature.

Rill Small brook, stream, channel, gully or rivulet.

Shuttering Wooden frame or boxing (also called formwork) used in the form of a mould when casting a concrete shape.

Spill stone Flat stone under a spout or waterfall, used to spread, deflect and break a heavy flow of water.

Squaring Technique of marking out with a set-square and or spirit-level so that one surface or structure is at right angles to another.

Submersible pump Water pump designed to work under water. Most small modern pond pumps are of the low-voltage submersible type.

Sump Pool or tank at the bottom end of a circulating system into which water drains. In many ways, a sump is a small or miniature version of a reservoir pool.

Tamping Using a length of wood to compact and level wet concrete.

Topsoil Top layer of soil, the best soil for planting.

Trial run Running through a procedure of setting out some part of a structure in order to discover whether or not the envisaged project or technique is feasible.

Underlay Soft material laid under the flexible liner; it could be anything from sand or layers of newspaper through to old carpet or purpose-made geotextile, as long as it will protect the flexible liner from sharp stones. See also Geotextile.

Water table Natural or constant level of water in the soil below which the water will not drain away. To find the water table, dig holes in various parts of your garden, at various times of the year (winter, spring, high summer and autumn) over say a three-year period, and keep a record of how far the surface of the water is below ground level.

Index

Acknowledgments

AG&G Books would like to thank Stephen Evans of **Golden Days Garden Centre**, Back Lane, Appley Bridge, Standish, Wigan, WN6 8RS, Tel. 01257 423355, goldendaysgardencentre@btconnect.com and Manchester Road, Cheadle, Cheshire, SK8 2NZ, Tel. 0161 4283098, goldendays@btconnect.com, www.goldendaysgardencentre.com for supplying the majority of photographs in this book. AG&G Books would also like to thank the RHS Gardens at **Hyde Hall**, Rettendon, Chelmsford, Essex, England and at **Wisley**, Woking, Surrey, England. Photographs: AG&G Books (cover and pages 2, 4, 6, 9, 16, 18, 20, 22, 24, 28, 32, 34, 42, 46, 52, 53 except TL, 55TC, 64 and 69), Golden Days Garden Centre (pages 3, 10, 32L, 34L, 48, 49, 50, 51, 53TL, 54, 55TL, TR and BL, 56, 58, 59, 60, 61, 62, 63 and 74), OASE (page 66) and Peter McHoy (page 55BR).